from FUNCTIONAL *to* PHENOMENAL

The Entrepreneur's Guide to Transforming Your Leadership and Business

JEVON WOODEN

From Functional to Phenomenal: The Entrepreneur's Guide to Transforming Your Leadership and Businesss

Copyright Jevon Wooden, 2025. All rights Reserved.

ISBNs: 979-8-218-59707-8 (hardcover)
        979-8-218-63349-3 (paperback)
        979-8-218-63350-9 (ebook)

Designed by Benjamin Kelley

CONTENTS

INTRODUCTION

 us indelibly. These moments often come unannounced, catching us in the midst of routine or chaos. They can be a simple realization or a life-altering event, shaping the very core of who we are. For some, it's a professional breakthrough; for others, it's a personal reckoning that redefines their path. Whatever form they take, these turning points become the axis on which our future pivots.

That day for me was November 12, 2016. I was stationed at Bagram Air Base in Afghanistan as a noncommissioned officer (NCO) in the US Army. For those of you who haven't had the pleasure, Afghanistan would be beautiful if not for war. It's a bit like California: flat, expansive desert in the South, lush and green in the West.

Built among the Hindu Kush Mountains, Bagram AFB has been an integral part of the American military presence in the region since the Cold War. The land surrounding the base is flat, as is everything around it, until you butt up against the staggering height of the mountains. In winter, the peaks are capped with snow. The expanse of the desert then spills into the villages beyond. These were villages where we built schools and dug water wells. We were doing the work of "winning hearts and minds."

On the base itself, we lived in a world of concrete. Everything was beige. The walls were beige. The sand was beige. Our uniforms—you guessed it: beige. Even the canteen coffee managed to be beige.

To keep our spirits up and stay fit, we did a lot of 5k runs. Fitness was a great distraction from war. The base had a beautiful gym. It was something of a sanctuary for me, a place to build camaraderie and let off steam.

That November morning was a clear, still day. The temperature was in the fifties, warm for that time of year, and the weather was perfect for running. Everyone was getting ready and lining up for our morning run at predawn. People were chatting and joking around. The mood was light—just another day. I had forgotten my glasses, so I quickly ran back to the barracks to grab them. No one wants a face full of sand or to be blinded by the desert sun.

As I was heading back to join the group from the barracks, a loud "BOOM!" shattered the peace of the morning. At first, I thought another of our trucks had accidentally gone into a ditch. One of the waste trucks had tipped over the other week—the sound and stench were awful. But then I saw everyone running back toward me. And I mean *running*. *Did the race start already?* I thought.

"Something detonated!" someone yelled as they dashed past me.

I was still three hundred meters away from the blast site, where the smoke was rising into the air. I heard people screaming and yelling. I sprinted toward the scene. There were bodies strewn about. Injured people writhed in pain. Blood and body parts were everywhere. It was a horrifying scene and one I will never forget.

Why did I run toward disaster and chaos? I don't attribute it to instinct—it's a commitment rooted deep within me. I'm the type of person who believes in the strength of duty and in putting others above self when the stakes are high. When I took the oath, it wasn't just words; it was a promise to stand ready, to prioritize the mission, and to protect those alongside me. In the military, we say, "Train as you fight," a phrase that carries weight beyond the battlefield. It means every day, every drill, is preparing us to be ready and decisive in moments of crisis. No matter your military occupational specialty (MOS), your number one job is infantry, to stand as the first line against threats. It's how I was trained—move in and neutralize the danger without hesitation. That training builds invaluable life skills; it shapes your values, crystallizing a sense of duty that runs deeper than fear. I snaked my way through the series of T-walls, tall concrete walls set up for security. The grey cement was splattered with sinew, flesh, and bone. As I approached the detonation site, I took a moment to survey what happened. The smoke was still clearing. People lay on the ground with shrapnel lodged in their shoulders, necks, and legs. Some were concussed and disoriented. There was mass confusion. Total pandemonium.

One woman in her thirties had taken shrapnel in her neck and shoulder. She was writhing in agony. I remember the panicked look in her eyes. My training kicked in. I said, "Hey, don't move, be still." Before you move someone, you are meant to feel behind them to see if there is an exit wound. I moved my hand gently to the back of her shoulder. There was no exit wound, but she was losing a lot of blood and needed medical attention immediately.

"Just get me out! Get me out!" she yelled. She was probably wondering if she would make it and fearing the worst. (I believe she pulled through in the end.)

The hospital was a mile away, and I knew every second was critical. I helped the woman and whoever else I could get into transport vehicles. Then, I grabbed someone else from my unit, and we ran down to the hospital. I helped with triage where I could.

Later that day, we learned what happened. An Afghani contractor who had been working on the base for five years had slowly been smuggling in parts for building a bomb. Eventually, he managed to assemble one. He had decided that was the day. In the early morning hours in Afghanistan, it was November 12, but back home in the States, it was still Veteran's Day, 11/11. The irony wasn't lost on any of us. To many, November 11 is a day of honor, remembrance, and gratitude for those who served. It felt almost poetic, yet chilling that the act was set against this backdrop of recognition and respect. The timing underscored the stark contrast between the solemn commemoration of service and the harsh reality of the dangers we faced. This coincidence made the moment heavier and served as a stark reminder that the sacrifices we commemorate aren't past stories. They are lived realities, unfolding even on days meant to honor those sacrifices. It was the job of the Contract Officer Representative, who is also a local, to supervise the workstations of local staff, but he hadn't picked up on the contractor's plot. Because the bomb had been brought in piece by piece, it was overlooked.

That morning, the contractor had compiled the bomb and put on a vest. He tried to get in the middle of the group gathering for the run to unleash the most carnage. Thankfully, some soldiers noticed him acting suspiciously and confronted him. One of them asked, "Hey! What are you doing?"

The bomber panicked, ran into one of the T-wall barriers, and detonated early. Had it not been for those soldiers running security, many more lives would have been lost.

And yet, the bomber killed six people and injured many others. Two of the soldiers killed had just arrived weeks ago. One I had been mentoring because he wanted to work in IT. He was interested in cybersecurity and was studying to get his certifications. The last time we spoke was in the gym. He asked me how I stayed so fit and joked that I must be skipping "Wing Wednesday." It was such an ordinary conversation. We had no idea it would be our last.

Although I survived that day physically unscathed, the mental and emotional toll was long-lasting, forcing me to work through it in therapy and struggle with some dark emotions. However, if there was a silver lining, it is that the experience altered the course of my life and put me firmly on the path to becoming a coach and, later, to focus on business and executive coaching.

Now, I'm grateful that I can spend each day doing what I do best: helping leaders and entrepreneurs thrive and grow their businesses.

The 5Y Framework

I came up with the 5Y Framework as a way to help service-based business leaders embrace the entrepreneurial journey with clarity and confidence. There are any number of coaching frameworks out there, but I wanted something new and different. I wanted something that incorporated everything I learned about the importance of connecting with people, giving people a sense of purpose, and doing everything you can to have a positive impact so I could use that as I grew my own business.

The "Y" is a play on words. To advance, you must ask "Why?" at every step. That's how you attain clarity and confidence. But the five "Ys" also refer to five key elements of the framework:

1. *Yardstick:* How do you measure success?
2. *Yield:* How are you going to hit your goal?
3. *Yare:* Yare is a boating term that refers to ease of use and maintenance. So, how do you make things easy for your business?
4. *Yoga:* How can you make your business flexible, strong, and scalable so that your business can thrive and survive no matter the circumstances?

5. *Yearn:* How can you turn customers and employees into evangelists for your brand? The best marketing is word of mouth, and you want people yearning for your brand.

By implementing the 5Y program, entrepreneurs can earn more revenue with less effort. It is an essential framework for business leaders, owners, C-suite executives, and key decision-makers. This book focuses on service-based businesses, which generally don't have to deal with supply chain logistics, making them more flexible and adaptable, but the information can be applied to any business and industry.

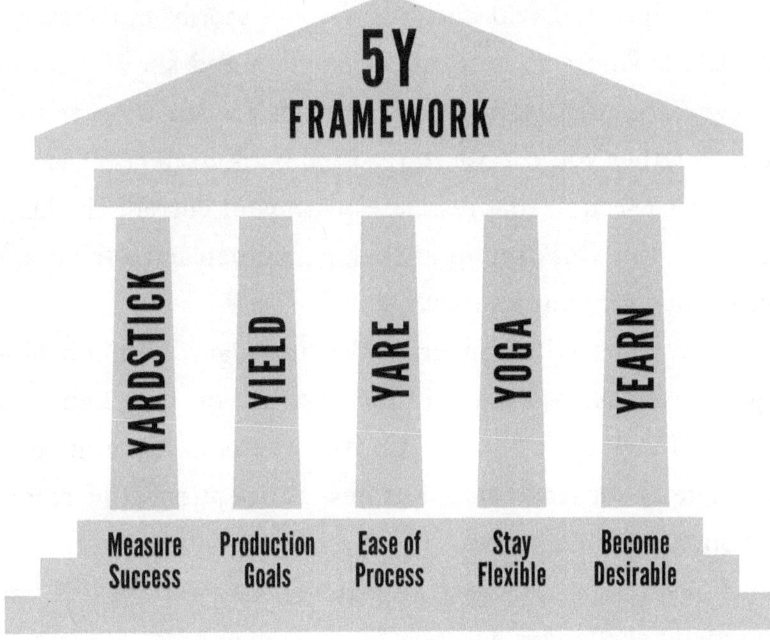

In this book, we'll look comprehensively at each element of the 5Y Framework and break each one down to understand how they can work for your business and your team. There is no stone left unturned. The book is organized into seven sections, including the Intro and Conclusion. The other five represent a fundamental pillar of the 5Y Framework and span fourteen chapters. This structure is intentional and designed to guide you through a logical progression where each chapter builds on the insights and strategies from the previous one. However, I understand that the journey of leadership and growth isn't always linear. That's why each chapter is also written to stand alone, allowing you to open the book to any page and find actionable guidance and inspiration when you need it most.

A big part of what I teach is the importance of storytelling in leadership. So, I will also share some stories you can apply to YOUR business to motivate your team and show them how it works. The methods I use have been proven time and time again. Whether you choose to read the book from cover to cover or jump to a section that resonates with your current challenges, I hope that this work serves as both a roadmap and a reliable reference guide for your journey.

And if you're still wondering *Who is this guy*, I am a business growth strategist, speaker, author, and, as you now know from the story I've just told you, a US Army veteran. I am incredibly passionate about leadership, business strategy, effective communication, marketing, technology, and helping motivated individuals and businesses achieve their goals. Throughout my life, I have faced many challenges and obstacles. I emerged stronger, wiser, and more determined to uplift others. I felt a calling to help others overcome their own obstacles and reach their full potential. In pursuit of this mission, I earned my master's degree in cybersecurity from Fordham University and my MBA from the Robert H. Smith School of Business at the University of Maryland. Drawing on my twelve years of experience in the military, I honed my expertise in all aspects of leadership and mindset under the highest possible stakes. And I've helped numerous clients generate more revenue with less effort using my innovative 5Y Framework. I firmly believe in the importance of mindset when facing challenging circumstances, and that one can do more with less by implementing a solid strategy and prioritizing good mental health. My business growth and development ideas have been featured in top publications such as *Entrepreneur, Fast Company, Foundr, Forbes,* and *Verizon.*

In addition to my academic background, I'm qualified because I've done it. I've led businesses in the boardroom, served as a leader in the field as an Army NCO, and am a business owner myself, so I know the ups and downs and trials and tribulations of running a business. I have a strategic, tactical mindset. I've been through tough economic times and survived Covid-19, so I understand uncertainty. I also have numerous marketing certifications and am a member of the American Marketing Association and the Digital Marketing Institute. I do nothing but study this stuff. I've walked the walk, and I want to help you do the same.

More importantly, I wrote this book from my unique perspective as a coach. It's one thing to learn how to grow a business from a businessperson, but it is another to learn how to grow a business from a business coach. In my work, I have helped copywriters, IT professionals, consultants, education entrepreneurs, marketing agencies, personal trainers, other coaches, authors, public speakers, and HVAC technicians—basically an array of different services across industries. The broad scope of clients has given me a comprehensive perspective and wide-ranging knowledge. No matter what corner of the business world you inhabit, this book will help you change how you approach and implement growth strategies.

I know that it takes more than metrics to achieve success. And I know that there are a lot of business books out there, but too many of them are weighed down by fluff or sugarcoating. This book candidly acknowledges the difficulties of building and growing a business. You *will* be faced with challenges. Being an entrepreneur or a business leader can be stressful and overwhelming at times. There is no point in running from that fact.

I want to help you face that reality and address common pitfalls, like skills gaps and lack of resources. Sometimes, you do need to put on your cape and run toward disaster. This book will provide actionable, strategic points you can implement immediately within your business and case studies showing that this stuff works. And it's also entertaining and engaging (or so my friends tell me).

I am passionate about sharing my blend of mindset and business coaching to help business leaders and entrepreneurs accomplish more while remaining true to themselves in the process. Whether you are looking to scale your business, build your brand, or navigate the ups and downs of entrepreneurship, this book aims to provide the support, insight, and expertise you need to achieve your dreams.

So, if you like the sound of that, this book is what you need. Let's dive in.

SECTION I: YARDSTICK

In the yardstick section, you will discover how to establish clear goals and measure success in a way that drives your business forward. This section will provide strategies for setting and aligning objectives, analyzing your business's unique strengths, and understanding your audience's needs. You'll explore how to stand out from the competition with effective differentiation techniques. The section also emphasizes the importance of using the right metrics to gauge progress, ensuring that you're not just moving but moving in the right direction.

CHAPTER 1: IDENTIFYING GOALS

I LEARNED THE IMPORTANCE OF GOAL SETTING THE SAME WAY I LEARNED MANY OF THE lessons of my younger years: the hard way. At the age of seventeen, I was facing seven years in prison. I wasn't a bad kid, but I found myself hanging with the wrong crowd on a night when I thought I was just going to see a movie with a guy I worked with at the local grocery store. We met up with two of his friends, and they went on a joyride, messing with innocent people. Although I never got out of the car that night, the officers said someone identified me. I was arrested five minutes walking distance from my house. I knew that was not the path I wanted to take, and thankfully, I never had to go down that road. I finished high school, but I couldn't afford to go to college. I stayed home and worked two full-time jobs. They kept me busy and out of trouble, and I saved as much as possible. My goals were simple: stay out of jail and don't die. But that was not enough. I knew I had to reassess. I didn't just want to survive; I wanted to thrive. I wanted to *live* and enjoy life.

I reviewed what I had (which was not a lot of anything—not a lot of money and not a lot of experience), and I analyzed my options. What *can* I do? That led me to the military. The military allowed me to learn, travel, and experience things I could not have otherwise. Some people told me I was crazy and tried to talk me out of it, but I knew I needed to do something different if I wanted to make something of myself. The goals I set—to live and thrive—drove me.

In this chapter, we'll outline simple steps to help you identify the right goals for your business. First, you'll need to thoroughly analyze your business and identify your key objectives and KPIs, clearly define your target audience, understand their needs and expectations, and align your goals with your brand values and mission. Then, you will need to implement tools and processes to measure your results. This includes setting up a tracking and reporting system to monitor your progress toward achieving your goals, using data and analytics to measure the effectiveness of your marketing campaigns and customer engagement strategies, and continuously evaluating and optimizing your approach based on insights and feedback from customers and stakeholders. We'll examine each of these steps and illustrate these concepts with some stories from my own experience and those of my clients.

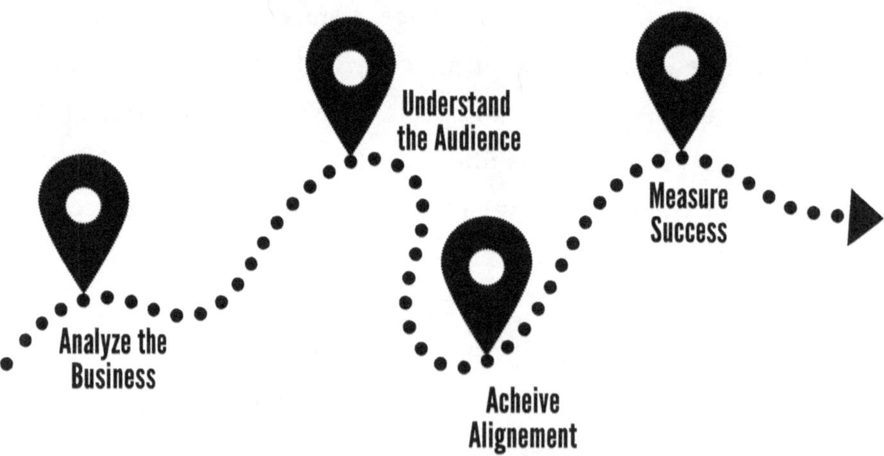

Set Your Sails for Success

The "yardstick" might be the most familiar of the 5Y Framework. You need to know how your business measures up—how far or close you are to the goal—so you know what strategy or course of action to take. But how do you know what the *right* goal is for your business?

To put it another way, imagine you're captaining a sailboat. The first thing you must do before lifting the anchor and setting sail is determine your destination. This will inform where to set your course, how you position your rudders, whether to hoist your sails—everything you need to make a plan of action. If you fail to set a proper goal, you will float aimlessly, a boat without a port in sight. Now, if you're stressed out, maybe it sounds relaxing to drift along with the tide, but I doubt you will be feeling very relaxed if you end up out to sea, totally lost, or even worse, shipwrecked on some proverbial desert island (RIP Blockbuster and Tower Records).

You need to have a destination—a goal—in mind that you can work toward. Goal setting is critical if you want to avoid wasting time and resources and minimize risk. As the saying goes, a ship is safe in harbor, but that's not what ships are built for. If you want to succeed, you need a destination beyond the safety of your home port. For your business, that means setting goals that will grow your business beyond the horizon of the status quo. Let's take it step by step and see what you need to set smart goals for your business.

We'll start with the #1 most important goal: *Analyze Your Business and Identify Objectives.* It's crucial to begin here to establish a strong foundation, understanding where your business currently stands and what objectives will propel you forward. From there, we'll move on to goal #2: *Understand Your Audience.* This step ensures that your strategies resonate with the people who matter most—your customers and stakeholders. Goal #3 is *Achieving Alignment,* which focuses on ensuring that your team and resources are unified toward shared objectives. Goal #4 is *Measuring Your Success,* where we'll cover the key metrics and tools you need to track progress and stay on course. Finally, goal #5 is *Optimize Your Approach,* where you'll learn how to refine your strategies based on data and insights to keep your business adaptable and competitive.

Analyze Your Business and Identify Objectives

The first step is to get clear on why you want to accomplish a goal. The goals you set for your business should be data-driven. Metrics and analytics are the sleeping giants of most companies. So, the first port of call is to conduct a thorough analysis of your business and identify your key objectives and performance indicators (KPIs). Start by reviewing your company's historical performance. This includes looking at sales, revenue, expenses, and profit margins. Equally important are customer acquisition costs, conversion rates, and retention rates. These metrics will help measure your progress toward your objectives and make data-driven decisions.

To know what objectives are most relevant to your success, learn from your history. Historical performance tells you what services are your best sellers, what your flagship service or product is, and where your marketing dollars are working hardest. (Hopefully, you are tracking all this; otherwise, you will have another issue!) Easy-to-use tools like Google Trends and Talkwalker Alerts can help make sense of your data. They show when your company is mentioned on social and traditional media, how effective your marketing strategy is, and which marketing lanes serve your company best. They can even help determine which clients might be potential ambassadors for user-generated content. Who are the repeat clients that you should cultivate further?

In small business, every dollar counts. You'll also want to ensure your resources are going to the right places. Businesses generally have different service lines, and sometimes certain lines support others. Historical performance tells you which are winners and which can be excised, downsized, or revamped later. It is just as important to cut service lines that are not performing well as it is to grow those that are. You don't want dead weight dragging your sailboat down.

It is so important to know where your business is and how it's performing at every stage. It might seem straightforward, but I cannot tell you the number of companies I've worked with that only calculate their profits when it comes to tax time. They see their top-line revenue week to week or month to month, but they have no idea how much they're making (or spending) until

March or April rolls around! That's no way to run a business. You risk losing revenue if you operate that way.

Instead, reconcile and review accounts at least quarterly. This will help determine your breakeven point and realistic sales goals. To return to our sailboat metaphor, as you navigate the coast, check your position—where you think you are on the map—with the reality of where you are. That way, you can readjust if need be or simply keep on cruising.

"Know Thy Enemy and Know Yourself"

Lao Tzu might be one of the most quoted figures when it comes to strategy of any sort, including business—and with good reason. If you want to succeed, you need to analyze your competition. How do you measure up in comparison to similar businesses in your industry and market segment? Your competition tells you the market landscape, what is in demand, and the market tolerance for certain products and services. What is your competitor's intake process? How do they attract clients and customers? Are your competitors using quizzes to get more leads? How do your competitors funnel sales to their business?

Your competition also tells you what *doesn't* work. Use SEO tools like SEMRush or Answer the Public to gauge the effectiveness of different keywords and determine what to put on your website. See who is ranking higher than you and what they're trending for. Look at their website to figure out the keywords and how best to place them. These are important factors if you want to be considered a market leader in your industry, especially as a service business.

If you do exactly what your competitor does, why would clients choose your business over theirs? The goal is not to imitate but to identify your unique selling points and areas where you can differentiate yourself. We'll go into more detail in the following chapter on how to differentiate yourself from competitors, but for now, we'll stick with why it's important in relation to goal setting.

I wrote earlier about the people who tried to dissuade me from joining the military. They thought it was too risky. They were afraid of what might happen if I got deployed. Their advice came from a place of fear. I saw it differently. The way I looked at it, the situation I was already in was about as bad as it could get. I needed to differentiate myself from the people around me. I needed to do something different if I wanted to achieve my goal. While they were paddling a rowboat in circles on a swamp, I had my sights set on a three-mast sailboat destined for distant lands.

What Makes You Unique?

Many entrepreneurs are good with the "heart work" side of their operations. They are passionate and want to help people. But they overlook the business side of things, which I think we can all agree is pretty integral to, well, running a successful business. This is especially true of service providers.

To give you an example, I worked with an educational consultant, Tanya. She was a bubbly woman in her fifties who had retired from teaching to start a business aimed at keeping high school-age, at-risk youth out of trouble and getting them into college. She had so much she wanted to accomplish and had set so many goals for helping kids, but she didn't have any business-oriented goals. She had left teaching in pursuit of financial freedom, but she was doing so much labor in return for very little financial return, so much so that she worried whether she could retire when the time came, as she had put all of her savings into the business.

Her business model wasn't working. She was casting a wide net, just trying to get someone, anyone, to purchase her services, but her messaging was unclear. She had no idea how to find prospective clients and, more importantly, what to say to turn them into clients. She didn't know her unique selling proposition (USP). She turned to me as a business coach in a final effort to turn the ship around before she was forced to give up and go back to a nine-to-five. She had heard me speak at a conference and said, "Something about you, I want to work with you." She admired my transparency and vulnerability. In our first meeting, she cried. She was so overwhelmed. As she told me about her work, it was apparent how much she cared.

Through our work together, I helped her narrow that down and identify her USP. As it turned out, she understood the issues at-risk youth faced more intimately because she had dealt with them in parenting her own kid. Unlike a lot of her competitors, she had the *lived experience*, which led her to get involved with this vulnerable population in the first place. That meant that when she spoke to groups of students and parents or students and teachers, it resonated on a real level. It set her apart from her competitors.

So What About SWOT?

You are no doubt familiar with SWOT analyses, the bread and butter of business strategy. A SWOT analysis helps identify the strengths, weaknesses, opportunities, and threats (SWOT) for your business or even a specific project. It is critical for creating a roadmap or action plan, and just like looking at historical performance is an important part of your yardstick, so is the ability to identify internal and external factors that can impact your business.

I like that SWOT can also be a powerful tool for personal growth and leadership development. I use this a lot in my coaching. The outcomes of a SWOT analysis—discovery, growth, and transformation—are vital processes for the individual, too. It can be a tremendous tool for leadership development. To return to our sailboat on the sea, think of a personal SWOT analysis as a kind of compass to guide you in the right direction. What are the opportunities *you* have for growth?

The effect of leadership cannot be underestimated when it comes to the growth and success of your business. A good leader can shape their workforce and workplace for the better. Your leadership style will be reflected across your business and to your customers. Truly adopting a growth mindset can have amazing, compounding effects. For instance, opportunities—even small, often overlooked ones—can serve as sparks of hope that illuminate the path toward achieving greater, more significant goals.

What Metrics Matter Most?

We live and operate in a world of data. Nearly everything is tracked and counted. Every click, every link, every ad, how long we spend on a page, every purchase, every item added to a cart, our age, gender, marital status, our search history—it's an inexhaustible list. So, how do you separate the wheat from the chaff? What metrics matter for your business? Another way to frame this is by asking, *What results matter?* As we touched on earlier, an essential part of your yardstick is identifying your business's key performance indicators (KPIs), such as customer acquisition costs, conversion rates, and retention rates. These metrics will help you measure your progress toward your objectives and make data-driven decisions.

To return to Tanya's story, before I started coaching her, Tanya had been looking only at revenue, not expenses or profits. Her business won grants and contracts, but they were one-offs. She had no steady or sustainable income. And she wasn't "paying herself first." She would even take on projects for free, just so she could help. Her business was chronically running a deficit. And it's not easy to see all your money going right back out the door—especially when there isn't much coming in.

Together, we tweaked her business model to enable her to teach authorities and organizations, not just kids directly, which was different from what other educational consultants were doing. She was able to tie in with major organizations like the YMCA. Not only did that give her business a competitive advantage, it meant that she could have a greater impact by reaching a wider audience. It also meant she had access to organizations and nonprofits with much bigger budgets than her own. It was a win-win solution: she got income streams, and they were able to help at-risk youth.

For more ideas on identifying specific KPIs you can leverage for your business, check out FunctionalToPhenomenal.com.

Understand Your Audience

Step 2 of establishing your yardstick is to get crystal clear on who you're talking to and why you aren't "an option" but "THE option." You wouldn't try to sell a sailboat to a person living in a desert. (Trust me, I spent a long time living in the desert: zero sailboats). So, why would you waste valuable time, effort, and money trying to sell your services to customers who aren't interested? Instead, you want to clearly define your target audience and understand their needs and expectations. I like to do this by developing buyer personas to give me and my clients a clear understanding of customers' demographic information, behaviors, pain points, and motivations. We will talk about this in depth later on, but it's important to touch on it briefly here. Ask yourself, "Who is my audience?" To develop buyer personas, think about both demographics and psychographics that apply to your service. Imagine that you're talking to a real person. Give them a name, age, and background. For each service or product you have, create an avatar. Ask yourself where they shop, the websites they visit, and how much they make per year. Dive into the details. You need to put that person in front of you. To help do this and make sure you're on the right track, conduct market research to understand your customers' preferences, trends, and expectations for products or services in your industry.

Let's put it into practice with real-world examples:

Here's a step-by-step guide for creating an avatar for a specific product or service, with examples for a product (hair extensions) and a service (consulting):

Steps for Creating an Avatar:

1. **Identify Demographics**: Start with basic details such as age, gender, income level, and location.

2. **Define Psychographics**: Consider values, hobbies, and interests that align with your service.

3. **Outline Pain Points and Needs**: What challenges does this avatar face that your product or service solves?

4. **Understand Behavior**: Where do they shop? What websites do they visit? How do they engage with products or services similar to yours?

5. **Create a Backstory**: Make them feel real by giving them a name, background, and daily life scenario.

6. **Refine with Market Research**: Validate your avatar by conducting surveys or analyzing market data to ensure accuracy.

Example 1: Hair Extensions (shout out to my wife, Kenya, the best cosmetologist I know!)

Product: Premium Hair Extensions

- **Avatar Name:** *Monica*, a 28-year-old fashion blogger.

- **Demographics**: Female, lives in a metropolitan area, earns $60,000/year.

- **Psychographics**: Passionate about beauty and fashion, values high-quality and authentic products, frequently posts on Instagram and TikTok showcasing her style.

- **Pain Points and Needs**: Wants voluminous, natural-looking hair that can be styled easily for content shoots. Struggles with finding extensions that blend seamlessly and last long without damage.

- **Behavior**: Shops at high-end beauty retailers and visits beauty influencers' websites. Follows popular hairstylists and beauty brands on social media. Reads beauty blogs for tips and product reviews.

- **Backstory**: Monica is always looking for ways to elevate her personal brand and maintain her chic appearance. She spends hours researching and reviewing beauty products to keep up with trends that align with her content aesthetic.

- **Market Research**: Surveyed social media trends and feedback from beauty-focused forums to understand what buyers are looking for in hair extensions.

Example 2: Consulting Services

Service: Business Consulting for Small Enterprises

- **Avatar Name**: *John*, a 42-year-old owner of a small marketing agency.

- **Demographics**: Male, located in a suburban area, earns $120,000/year from his business.

- **Psychographics**: Ambitious and values efficiency, growth-oriented, spends free time reading business development books and attending webinars. Prefers strategic insights backed by data.

- **Pain Points and Needs**: Struggling to scale his business due to inefficient processes and team communication issues. Needs expert guidance to streamline operations and foster growth.

- **Behavior**: Regularly visits business news sites, listens to podcasts about entrepreneurship, and is part of online business forums. Attends local networking events to build partnerships.

- **Backstory**: John has built his agency from the ground up over the last decade but feels stuck in reaching the next level. He's seeking consulting that aligns with his goal to expand while maintaining quality service.

- **Market Research**: Analyzed feedback from small business owners and engaged in industry discussions to pinpoint their most pressing challenges.

Turning the Rudder

I worked with a young man, Sean, who wanted to be a personal trainer. He was a laid-back 24-year-old and former Division 1 college athlete. Not a big guy, but tenacious. He knew what he wanted and was mature beyond his years. He was aspirational and had something most lacked, which was a tremendous work ethic. He had been injured a lot playing college football and kept on going. He carried that mentality into his business.

"I want to help train young athletes, people like me," he said.

However, when he studied his client base, he found that it was mostly women booking sessions with him. They were a bigger demographic in the geographic area, and they liked the way he trained and the results he helped his clients achieve.

Sometimes, you need to pivot. In Sean's case, his customer data was pointing us in a different direction. So, we switched it up and leaned more heavily on that demographic. It made sense because college athletes tend to have their own trainers through their schools' training programs. Meanwhile, the young women in his area, mainly African American women in their mid-twenties to early thirties, were most interested in his services and had the time and disposable income to employ him. (Again, something he was less likely to get from broke college kids!) We also added group coaching to give his clients a sense of community and accountability, which was important to them. As a silver lining, that also shaved some hours from his workdays, which were too long. (We're talking 5 am to 8 pm—when I say this man had work ethic, I mean it!)

Knowing and understanding his audience empowered him to work smarter, not harder. There are easy-to-use, quick-to-implement tools available to help you do this. We will get into this in detail later on, but as you set goals, it's important to make sure they're the right goals.

Go to the Source & Gamify Engagement

One of the most accurate and easiest ways to develop a deeper understanding of your customer is simple: ask them. Use social media and customer surveys to gather feedback and insights from your existing customers. Get people engaged so they feel like they're a part of what you're building. You want customers to feel like your company "gets them." People are always searching for connection and purpose. People want to be heard.

Another way to learn about your customers is to analyze your competitors' customers. Then, you can identify gaps in their offerings that your business can fill. You can use forums like Reddit, Quora, Clutch, and Glassdoor to view users' comments on competitor companies, including complaints. You can glean differentiating factors and learn about what makes you stand out and what makes you *better*. Leverage that by touting it on your own page. (For instance, "There's always a human answering the phones.") If your primary competitors don't have an online or social media presence, you probably don't have much competition to worry about!

A great way to boost engagement is to gamify your outreach efforts. There is a reason why companies from Twitter to Tinder have started to gamify the user experience. Gamification has been shown to increase engagement and boost customer loyalty. It appeals to our human instincts and motivations, like the desire for a sense of purpose and accomplishment. Try creating leaderboards and offer giveaways. Reward customers with badges and develop referral programs. Most importantly, don't be boring! Make it fun.

Achieving Alignment

After you "Analyze Your Business and Objectives" and "Understand Your Audience," you can shift your focus to aligning your goals to your greater mission. You might think alignment belongs in the "yoga" section of this book, but it is an essential part of goal setting. Align your goals with your brand values and mission. Identify your brand's core values and mission statement to understand what your company stands for and how you want to make an impact.

And don't let the mission statement go stale. I review mine each year.   At the time of writing, our mission statement at BrightMind Consulting Group is as follows: At BrightMind Consulting Group, our mission is to empower leaders to reach their fullest potential through customized development programs, dynamic workshops, and impactful coaching. By seamlessly integrating emotional intelligence with actionable strategies, we inspire top talent, drive innovation, and cultivate meaningful collaboration. Our goal is to help our clients build a culture of care that transforms their organizations through the empowerment of their people.

As I expand, add new services, and evolve, my mission statement changes, too. If you're having trouble with that, ask yourself, What do I stand for? What are my non-negotiables? Do I want to have a social impact? Am I supporting a cause?" More and more consumers—and employees—want to patronize and support businesses that uphold their values. Communicate all that in your mission and values.

Your brand content should reflect that, too. If you're at a loss for articles to publish on your site, talk about your values and mission. It will keep your content fresh and attract clients with similar values and goals.

And you have to stick to those values. That might mean turning down a speaking gig or media appearance that could boost your profile. For instance, I had a prospect who aspired to be an Andrew Tate-type by starting some kind of sex-related business. He said we could make millions, but I just said, "I don't do that, bro." He may have been right about the money (I hope not), but sometimes you have to draw a line in the sand. Your integrity will matter to the clients you *do* work with.

Ensure your goals align with your brand values and mission statement so you can build a meaningful and purpose-driven business. Then, use your brand values and mission statement to guide decision-making and prioritize initiatives. Communicate with your employees and customers so they understand what you stand for and can advocate for your business. Everyone wants to feel a sense of purpose. Your business can deliver that to clients and employees if you have meaningful values that speak to them.

And the value of values is, well, invaluable. Achieving alignment can lead to higher productivity and employee satisfaction, improved financial performance, and superior customer experience. All goals you should be aiming for.

Measuring Your Success

Now that our business objectives, who we want to serve, and our goals as leaders align with the organization's values and mission, we can move to the fourth step of identifying how we measure success. Of course, the primary use of a yardstick is to measure. Now that you've done the hard work of gathering, comparing, and analyzing data, it's time to measure your success.

The first thing you'll want to do is set up a tracking and reporting system to monitor the progress toward achieving your goals. At the highest level, this means first identifying the relevant metrics and KPIs to track progress toward your goals, such as website traffic, conversion rates, social media engagement, customer retention, and revenue growth. Then, you can determine which tools and platforms for tracking and reporting will best suit your needs, such as Google Analytics, social media analytics tools, customer relationship management (CRM) systems, and marketing automation software. Finally, set up a dashboard or regular reporting system to ensure you have clarity on the performance of your marketing efforts and can make informed decisions based on the data.

This might all seem quite straightforward, but I've found through my work with clients that many businesses miss key opportunities when it comes to using these tools effectively. For example, a CRM is more than simply email management software; if used optimally, it's a whole data ecosystem. It can be used as a pipeline for tracking everything from cold and warm leads, recording who was opened and who was closed, and taking detailed notes on individual clients. In this case, it's about the quality and depth of your data as much as the quantity.

A Boatload of Tools

There is no shortage of tools that help track and measure what you need for your business. So, let's have a look at some of the most user-friendly options.

One of my favorite measurement tools is Google's free suite of tools, including Google Analytics and Search Console. These give you invaluable information like how many users or visitors to your site, how long they spend on the site or an article, your bounce rate, and whether your pages are being indexed—metrics that are super critical for any service business.

Many clients tell me, "I don't get much traffic."

So I ask them, "Do you know how much traffic you get per week?"

"I don't know," they say.

"Do you have Google Search Console set up?"

"No."

If that's the case, they are missing out on one of the most powerful (and free) tools for analyzing traffic. They don't know what is working on their site, what pages people are engaging with, and where potential clients are walking away. And while we're on the subject, be sure you own your domain! Owning your own domain name can boost your SEO by helping you rank higher on search results. It's also easier for customers to remember and adds a sense of professionalism and reliability.

Google Analytics also provides data on any paid ads you might be running. Marketing and advertising can substantially drain small businesses, so ensure that the money you spend is worth it. You need to know what kind of traffic, conversion rates, and real revenue you're getting from your ads. Google Analytics can also be tied to social media platforms like Facebook. Again, be sure your social media accounts for your business are set up correctly as business pages, as they offer different features from personal pages.

LinkedIn Creator Mode is another superb tool for service businesses. LinkedIn is *the* professional network online. Using Creator Mode to go live or post content will boost your visibility to potential prospects and partners. It can serve as an extension of your email list. Your content may even get featured in a LinkedIn newsletter, which will help skyrocket your visibility. Commenting on other people's posts and direct messaging potential partners can also help you connect with a wider audience. Using Creator Mode is a great way to kickstart your profile as a thought leader in your industry. I reach thousands of people this way each week.

If you want to grow your business, you will need leads. Today, there are marketing automation tools that can generate leads for your business. It's important to remember that when you do outreach, the point is not to sell, per se. Instead, you want to use that time to make a connection and start building a relationship. Do some background research so you can personalize your initial conversation. Then, on the call, ask about their goals and how you can help reach them. The measure of a good call can be as simple as, "I'm interested. Let's follow up in a week." A bad call is hearing, "I'm not interested," or "I'm retired." Make sure they know you're coming from a place of service and genuine connection.

You can and should track all this, but let the software do the work for you. Set up a workflow using your CRM, track cold, warm, and hot leads, and start to automate your touch point process. That leads us to our next means of measuring: dashboards.

Dashboard Data

Lastly, set up a dashboard or regular reporting system to ensure that you have visibility into the performance of your marketing efforts and can make informed decisions based on the data. Your dashboard should tie together your CRM data and automated processes to give you a more granular view. For example, if you send four emails (one initial and three follow-ups, as I like to do), your dashboard can show you the results of that email campaign. Likewise, if you A/B test, you can see which version was opened more or generated more engagement.

Your dashboard will also give you an at-a-glance view of how close you are to achieving your goals. Make sure you have a clear goal in mind, a clear strategy for achieving it, and a clear message for communicating it. For instance, if your goal is to boost traffic to your website, then your KPIs will be very different than if your goal is to increase conversion rates. Everything you do should align with the goal of your campaign.

Optimize Your Approach

Never let your business strategy stagnate. The fifth step, "Optimizing Your Approach," is more of an iterative process to continuously improve your strategy and tactics. Continuously evaluate and optimize your approach based on insights and feedback from customers and stakeholders. We've already established that you need a process for gathering feedback and insights from customers and stakeholders through surveys, focus groups, and other mechanisms. Use that process to identify common threads and patterns. Analyze feedback and data to identify areas for improvement in your marketing and engagement strategies. For instance, if call times are too long, find a way to shorten them. Are you taking too long to get back to prospects? Tighten up the timeline for follow-ups or automate the process.

My services are always in beta mode, always evolving and improving based on customer feedback. For example, when I first began coaching, my program was 12 weeks, but clients said it was too long. They had trouble sticking with it and maintaining focus. In response, I created a mid-tier six-week program, which filled the need and increased the number of enrollments.

Be sure to use insights gleaned from the data to optimize your approach and meet the needs and expectations of your target audience. As another example, I noticed that enrollment for my coaching courses was lower than my target goal. After conducting surveys with past and potential clients, I found it was because they couldn't always commit to specific timelines and thought they might miss important stages of the course. So, instead of cohorts that all start at once, I offer rolling enrollment. Clients can start at any point, and all the lessons are recorded, so they can watch later if they miss a class. After adjusting the enrollment style, I experienced an uptick in sales—which I knew because I was diligently tracking everything on my dashboard!

As you can see, data is your friend. If you have clear goals, set your objectives, gather the data, and continuously optimize your strategy and processes, you'll be set up for success. In the next chapter, we'll take a closer look at differentiating your business from your competitors.

NOTES

CHAPTER 2: DIFFERENTIATING FROM COMPETITORS

COMPETITION CAN TAKE MANY FORMS. FOR MANY OF US, OUR FIRST EXPERIENCE WITH competition is through sports, fighting to win each game or that golden trophy at the end of the season. There is also internal competition—the ways we compete with ourselves to make ourselves better. And there's external competition. We all hope to corner the market, but let's be honest: most service-provider sectors are saturated these days. Nevertheless, that's not necessarily a bad thing. You can use competition to grow your business by leveraging your competition's weaknesses to your advantage and learning from their strengths. And it's a win for your customers as well, who will benefit from greater innovation, fairer prices, and better value and service for customers.

We touched on this subject in Chapter 1, but it's a particularly important part of the yardstick, so let's take a closer look at how you can leverage competition to your advantage.

External Competition: Be the First to the Table

My earliest exposure to competition and the need to differentiate from competitors was at home. This may come as a surprise to many of you, but I was raised in a polygamous Muslim family. My mom was one of two wives. In my household, I was the middle child of five, so every meal was a competition. My siblings teased me and called me "chipmunk cheeks" because I would eat absolutely anything my momma put on the table. My favorite was chicken and dumplings. And let me tell you this: "Be the first one to the table" is great advice not only for getting the lion's share of chicken and dumplings but for business as well! Scoop up as much of the share as possible before your competitor knows you're in the kitchen. And before you all give me the side-eye, I always made sure my siblings ate, too, especially my little sisters.

We were a tight-knit family, but we learned how to do without. Our house in Rochester, New York, was built in the 1930s, so something always needed to be fixed or repaired. It was kind of falling apart, but it *was* 70 years old—most of us will be falling apart by that age. If the electric bill wasn't paid, we'd have to light candles and burrow under blankets in the dead of winter.

As you might imagine, the two-household situation also created competition with the other household. The other house was better resourced and maintained. I often felt like we got the short end of the stick, and I always believed my mom deserved better. I would often ask myself, *Why is Mom dealing with this? Is this love?* She was awesome, a beautiful woman, and incredibly nurturing. She cared tremendously for each of her children. Her husband, who was not my father, rotated days between the two families, joining us every other day but never taking the time to connect with us.

And yet, our home was not as chaotic as you might think. We all had our own rooms. When I hit my teen years, I was in the streets more often than at home, playing basketball or hanging out with friends. And there was a lot of love. We'd watch movies together and do things as a family. Sometimes, it was as simple as sitting on the porch together and watching the world go by. We valued what we did have.

You learn how to be resourceful when resources are limited. And while that might sound like a struggle, it was also an opportunity to learn. I learned everything I could from my siblings. What time do I need to wake up to be the first in the bathroom? (You didn't want to be the last one because you were guaranteed to take a cold shower.) What do I need to do to get good grades and be successful?

Your story might look different from mine (or maybe it's all too familiar), but however you grew up, we all have something to learn from the experience of competition. And any business is sure to face its moments of adversity and challenge. So, what is the takeaway from this? You must learn to make the most out of everything—including your competition. Be resourceful. Be resilient. These strengths will serve you endlessly as a business owner, entrepreneur, or leader of any kind. If you don't want to be scraping the bottom of the pot for the last dumpling, you need to beat out the competition.

Internal Competition

It is not enough to think about and respond to external competitors. Motivation and drive come from within. Change, development, and growth are all positive byproducts of internal competition.

I started high school in 1999. I was only 13 years old since I had skipped the sixth grade. School came easily for me. I didn't try hard because I wasn't motivated. I'd hang out with my friends, roll dice, get my hair braided—I did everything except study. Still, I earned a 3.5 GPA.

After my first semester in high school, the global studies teacher, Ms. Chazan, said, "I see great potential in you. You have the best grades in the class. You barely show up, but when you do, you demonstrate aptitude." Now, truth be told, I was really only showing up to that class because there was a cute girl I liked. I'd tell my best friend, Rese, "Hey, if I came on time, I could've sat next to Dominique." But Ms. Chazan's comment was the first time I heard that kind of praise, someone saying, "You can do more than you think you can." (I learned later that words of affirmation are my love language—if you're familiar with that framework.) She encouraged me to take Advanced Placement courses, motivated me, and kept me on track by pushing me to reflect inwardly and think about my goals.

I come back to this experience often when I feel demotivated or directionless. As we discussed in the previous chapter, the yardstick is about having clearly defined goals, a mission, and values to guide your action. We can be our own worst enemies, falling into a sense of helplessness or laziness. When this happens, find what sparks that sense of internal competition. What drives you? What motivates you? Try gamifying your goals. Use your yardstick and set rewards for each metric you meet.

You can also use internal competition in conjunction with a SWOT analysis—which we discuss in detail in the following pages—to learn and grow from knowing your strengths and weaknesses. In some sense, this is what every business does year to year when we set goals for growth. We want to beat our sales, acquisitions, and retention rates—whatever the yardstick may be—from the previous year or quarter. We are always competing against ourselves first.

Putting the "You" in USP

We hear a lot about "unique selling proposition" (USP), but what exactly does it mean? How are you different? What makes you stand out? In terms of the yardstick, how do you measure up against competitors? It might be your branding, how you implement a product or solution, or the lifestyle appeal of your service. There are a hundred different ways to differentiate yourself.

Take the case of Apple vs. Samsung. Their smartphones both essentially perform the same functions, but both have unique brand elements, from messaging to marketing, from tech specs to user experience. Apple differentiates itself through its sleek, minimalist design, seamless integration across its ecosystem (iPhones, MacBooks, iPads, and Apple Watches), and a reputation for premium quality and innovation. On the other hand, Samsung is known for its cutting-edge technology, such as high-resolution displays (such as AMOLED screens), customizable user interfaces, and versatile hardware options like the Galaxy Fold. These differentiators create distinct experiences for users. Apple users appreciate the simplicity, exclusivity, and status symbol associated with the brand, while Samsung users value flexibility, advanced technology, and the ability to customize their devices. This clear differentiation fosters brand loyalty: Apple users rarely defect to an Android phone, and Samsung users would never line up for the newest iPhone.

If there are thousands of competitors in your industry, finding and communicating your USP is challenging. Perhaps it's your unique service line or how your customer service is set up. It's important to keep in mind that the USP should be aimed at and benefit your customer, not you. Customers are interested in how you can help *them*. What problem can you solve for *them*? What service can you provide *them* that will make their life easier? What can you do to improve or affirm *their* lifestyle?

Starbucks is a great example of this. For a company that essentially just sells coffee, they have found a USP to sell more than coffee. They sell an upmarket lifestyle image— premium coffee and food in a chic yet comfortable environment—at a premium price.

Virtually every client I have worked with has struggled with this at some point. Many lose sight, distracted by what others are doing. And there is a fine line here: knowing what's happening with your competitors is important, but you don't want to lose sight of your own goals.

When I got to high school, I realized I was "doing without" in ways other kids weren't. I saw other kids wearing cool gear or the latest jerseys. (That was *the thing* to have in the late 90s/early 2000s. If you know, you know.) And suddenly, I wanted that. I let the environment of competition change my mindset. I thought, *I want what they have.*

If I could go back in time, I would tell my younger self to reassess, just like I do with business clients today. I would ask that kid, "Does this align with who you really are and who you want to be?" Nine times out of ten, that goal probably does not align with your own mission and values. Back then, I was attracted by the lure of material possessions. It was a kind of vanity. And it distracted me from my real goal of making a success of myself and getting out of Rochester.   Eventually, I did get it together—I learned to realign my focus, prioritize my true values, and channel my ambition into meaningful actions that set me on the path to growth and fulfillment.

In business, taking on your competitors' goals can be a distraction. If you see the competition featured in a publication, then you covet that—even though it may not align with your goals. The best thing to do is return to the subject at hand: the first "Y," the yardstick. Ask yourself, "What am I looking to accomplish and why?" If you get distracted, you'll end up running toward the wrong goal line.

As an example, I worked with one client who owned an electrician services company in the Houston area. Electrician services businesses are local by nature; you aren't going to service someone's Malibu mansion if you're based in Mobile, Alabama. This client used to see ads for his competitors everywhere. He was hung up on the fact that they were running ads on major news networks and national platforms. "I see 'em all over the place, and it's driving me insane! I want *my* ads to be every-where!" he said.

So, I asked, "What separates you from them?"

Well, it turned out that not only did he have qualifications that his competitors lacked, but his primary USP was that he was a smaller company, not a national chain. I encouraged him to lean in on being smaller, more responsive, and reliable. I suggested that he communicate his status as a small business. Who doesn't love a local mom-and-pop shop? Instead of advertising to a national audience, his business would be better served by using his more limited marketing budget toward features in the *Houston Business Journal* or on local news stations, which were far more relevant and likely to reach his potential customers. Relationship building would be more likely to amplify the profile of his small business than a national marketing campaign. And that pivot translated into a better marketing strategy focused on local exposure.

So, we know why setting yourself apart from the competition is important, but how do you accomplish that? What should your next steps be?

Conduct a Competitive Analysis

The first step is to the heart of what makes your competitors who they are by conducting a competitive analysis to identify their strengths and weaknesses.

First off, how do you know who your competitors are? Let's take Airbnb as an example. Their obvious competitor would be similar platforms like VRBO, but to conduct a thorough competitive analysis, they would also need to include hotel chains and individuals who rent out homes privately. Additionally, Airbnb offers an "Experiences" line of services that competes with tour operators and private companies, which introduces competitors like Booking.com or Expedia into the mix.

To conduct your own analysis, find companies that offer similar services or products to a similar audience. Geography and demographics also matter. Keep in mind that you need to be realistic about who your competitors are. For instance, I don't see Deloitte as my competitor, even though we offer the same kind of service. Deloitte is a huge firm on an altogether different scale, serving a different clientele.

Once you have identified who to include in your analysis, dig into the market as deeply as possible. Gather data on your competitors, including their product offerings, pricing, marketing strategies, and customer reviews. In the last chapter, we discussed developing buyer personas to help you better understand your customers. Now, you want to do something similar with your competitors.

Your competitors' websites can provide a wealth of data about who they are, what they provide, how they operate, who they serve, what they charge, and more. For example, if their Google reviews are bad, what are people saying about them, and how can you avoid that? If you want to take your research a step further, set up a call with them. Sign up for their newsletter. Find out first-hand how they interact with prospective clients. How many touches do they make with prospects, and how often? Are they upselling or down-selling? Do they have an online presence or a thriving social media following? What is the tone of their social media content? Do they have dedicated followers—and can you poach some of them? What keywords are they using? How often do they post new blog content? How is their customer service set up? Don't be afraid to get granular. And be sure to set up a tracking system for all the information you gather.

Then, take all that rich data and analyze it. Identify patterns and trends to help you understand your competitors' strengths and weaknesses. Compare everything you are doing with how they do it. You can find digital tools to help you do this at FunctionalToPhenomenal.com.

A Fresh Take on SWOT

Another tool for finding your USP is our old friend SWOT. Just like how we turned the buyer personas outward into competitive analysis, this time, we're turning the traditional SWOT inward. One thing I have found consistently helpful across the board with clients is getting them to conduct a SWOT analysis on themselves, not just their companies. It's an excellent tool for identifying how you can leverage your personality or personal brand to determine what distinguishes you as a leader. You have to find out what makes you "you."

For example, one of my favorite coaches is LaTisha Styles. She's an introvert, and she leans into that. She talks about it openly. Her early mentors advised her not to be herself, to overcome or suppress her introversion, and to "get out there and network" in order to grow her business. That didn't work for her. So, she emphasized digital marketing and other channels that are more introvert-friendly. What others saw as a weakness, she leveraged into a strength. And her success shows how important authenticity is to any audience. It's better to be a real introvert than a fake extrovert.

Moreover, an organization will reflect the personality of its leader. If you don't know yourself, it can be hard to cultivate a cohesive brand or corporate identity, which is critical if you want to cultivate brand loyalty and boost employee and customer retention.

We'll talk more about the personal SWOT in a later chapter, but for now, keep in mind that it can be used to assess various aspects of your business, including your competition and yourself.

Develop and Differentiate

Once you have completed your analysis, use the insights gained to develop a strategy to differentiate your brand from competitors and capitalize on gaps in the market. Conduct a SWOT analysis to identify your brand's strengths, weaknesses, opportunities, and threats. Use the analysis to identify your brand's USPs and value propositions that set you apart from competitors. Then, focus on the strengths and opportunities identified in the analysis and build marketing strategies around them.

Like so much in life, the most important part of all this is communication. You want to get your message across to your audience! Communicate your differentiation clearly and consistently across all marketing channels and touchpoints. Develop clear and consistent brand messaging that communicates your USPs and value propositions. Use a mix of marketing channels to reach your target audience and reinforce your messaging. And lastly, ensure that your messaging and branding are harmonious across all channels, including social media, email marketing, website, and in-store experience.

Your messaging should convey your USP, implicitly or explicitly. If customer service is a selling point, communicate that. Tell your audience you have a "99 percent customer satisfaction score," a thousand five-star ratings, or that you have been recognized by Glassdoor as Best Place to Work. If you got it, flaunt it. Convey your message on your blog, website, social media, paid ads—*everywhere*. And convey it in engaging ways. A quiz might appeal to one client, and a podcast or video might be the way you reach another.

I rely heavily on social media to communicate my USP. I am very transparent on social media. My storytelling is one differentiator. I'm authentic—always me. I bring a lot of energy, but I don't act too polished or high and mighty (my humble beginnings help keep my ego in check). I am responsive to clients and prospects, personable, and real. I also don't act like I know everything; I turn my vulnerability into a strength. This book is a prime example: I'm sharing a lot of my own history as part of the larger story of how to grow your business.

So, use every available option and tool to turn your competition into an advantage. Look at both internal and external competition. Follow the steps to finding your USP and using SWOT analysis to improve your business and yourself. Put all that data to good use in defining your goals. Now you have your yardstick.

Once that is in place—and you have all the measurements and metrics needed to set a strategy—let's have a look at the next "Y" of our 5Y Framework. In the following section, we'll dissect the "yield," or how to achieve the outcomes and goals you set with your yardstick.

Section Summary:

- Goal setting is essential for steering your business toward success.

- A clear destination ensures you allocate time and resources effectively.

- Goals should align with your brand values, mission, and customer needs.

Action Steps:

1. Define 3-5 measurable goals for your business.

2. Identify key performance indicators (KPIs) that will track progress toward these goals.

3. Set up a system to measure and review your progress regularly.

4. Evaluate whether your goals align with your business's core mission and values.

NOTES

SECTION II: YIELD

Once you identify your yardstick as your key measurement for success, the next step is determining what levers the business can pull to produce your desired outcomes. This is the "yield" of the 5Y Framework. Identifying the right levers involves examining the various factors that will contribute to your success and identifying areas for improvement. We will examine two main factors through the lens of yield: people and technology. In this chapter, we are going to focus on people.

CHAPTER 3: PEOPLE

WITHOUT SOUNDING TRITE, IT'S TRUE WHAT THEY SAY: PEOPLE ARE THE HEART OF ANY business. This includes both your employees and your customers. Your employees' dedication, innovation, and expertise are among the greatest assets and advantages your company can have. Can you attract and retain top talent to work for you? Are you able to appeal to new customers and build your base? Can you grow your client list and expand your sphere of influence? People expect more from a company these days. They want purpose and fulfillment. For your employees and your clients, that means listening to their needs, goals, and desires. What do they need to be happy, and how can you deliver that? How can you, as a leader, guide people toward identifying and pursuing their goals?

A Night at the Movies

It was February 2003. I was living in Rochester, NY, and it was cold as hell. I had plans to go to the movies with my homeboy, Dave, who I worked with at the grocery store. Dave was a tall, fair-skinned guy with braces and braids—a self-proclaimed "ladies' man" who was always rocking the latest fashion. On our way to the movies, we stopped at the store, and Dave ran into a couple of other guys he knew.

"We're gonna roll. We all gonna go out," Dave said.

I didn't know the other guys, but Dave was cool and never got in trouble, so I thought, *No problem, whatever. It's just a movie. What's the worst that could happen?*

Well, these two guys turned out to be complete fools. Instead of going to the movies, we spent the night riding around, and these guys kept jumping out and punching random people unprovoked.

I didn't want any part of it. I was like, "What in the hell? Take me home. Y'all are crazy."

I dozed off on the way to my house. We were five minutes away, and the cops pulled up behind us. I woke up to flashing lights.

"Step out of the car," I heard the officer say.

One of the officers put me in the back of his car. "So, do you want to tell me what was going on?" he asked me. He was putting on his best "good cop" performance, trying to win me over.

"No idea, officer," I said. "I was asleep."

"You're going to jail, son," the officer told me that night.

I was stunned.

They took us to the station. I was in the interrogation room for hours. It was freezing. I'm fairly certain they had the heat off—in February, in upstate New York, if you recall. This undoubtedly helps encourage people to do whatever is necessary to get out of that icebox. When they finally came back to the room, I was told they wanted to charge us for assault and robbery. I hadn't hit anyone or taken anything. I hadn't even left the car.

Don't get me wrong—I wasn't entirely innocent. Around that time, I had taken up robbing drug dealers. This was the Rochester version of Robin Hood. In our neighborhood, drug dealers were the closest thing we had to the upper class. They had cash, flashy cars, and more resources than they knew what to do with. In contrast, my family was poor, and our poverty was of the kind that could make your heart heavy and your life harder. There were too many mouths to feed, too many dreams to nurture, and too many problems to solve with too few resources.

As time went on, things got tougher, and the dreams we harbored as kids started to fade. We had to look for other ways to make ends meet. That's when sticking up dealers came into the picture. I know it sounds dangerous, even immoral. It was. But it also seemed like a logical choice in an illogical world, a world where selling drugs was normal, where men had multiple wives and children scattered around the city like puzzle pieces they never intended to complete.

I wasn't robbing people out of malice or greed. I was a kid trying to survive in a world that didn't seem to want me to. I did it for food. I did it for school supplies. I did it for my younger siblings who I wanted to offer a better life. I did it because I felt that society had forgotten about us, left us in the gutters to fend for ourselves. And I was seventeen. I didn't fully grasp the risks or the repercussions. I never thought about it until I landed in jail—for an altogether different crime.

I got my one call and phoned my mom, Pat. It was 3 am, and she was groggy when she picked up. "You're in jail? What do you mean? What's going on?" she asked in a panic.

I explained as quickly as I could.

"Do you need a lawyer?"

"Yes," I said.

"Just stay strong, Jevon," she told me.

And that was all we were able to say to each other before they cut me off. I was in there for a couple of weeks with no other contact. My mom somehow managed to get me a lawyer despite being broke. She put the house up as collateral, which meant risking homelessness for all of us if I missed any of my court dates.

I was only 17 years old. The fact she put the house up conveyed how much she cared about me. Letting people know you value them can change the trajectory of what they're willing to do for you and your company. Sometimes, it's as small as a "thank you" or remembering someone's birthday. Sometimes, it's as big as a house.

Power to the People

So, how can you demonstrate that you value your employees and what really matters to them? Gone are the days of throwing a neat little benefits package at your employees and hoping they stay. People need purpose. We crave meaning in our lives. And with so much of our time spent working, that means that people want their work to feel purposeful and meaningful. That, in turn, means that your business needs a social cause, a bigger picture that people can get behind.

At one point in my career, I worked as a tech employee, and I *hated* it. I wanted to do more. I had ideas but no outlet for realizing them. No matter how many times I went to my manager with ways to improve sales or processes, nothing changed. I felt unfulfilled, and because of that, most days, I just dialed it in. It took someone else pointing me in a different direction to turn that boat around, but we'll get to that story later. The bottom line is you do not want people "quiet quitting"—people taking up space in your company who do not want to be there and don't meaningfully contribute to your growth. It's not good for you or them.

There are three main pieces of the people puzzle: hiring, training, and culture. We'll look at each in the sections below and talk through how to ensure you have the right people doing the right job with the proper support to create a culture of growth and fulfillment.

Measure Twice, Cut Once

You can't bake a cake without the right ingredients, and you can't build a great company without the right people. Your job as a leader, business owner, or entrepreneur is to hire the best talent you can. To do this, you must offer competitive compensation and benefits to attract and retain top talent. Then, hire and train employees who are skilled and experienced in their roles. This involves identifying the specific skills and experience required for each role within your organization and conducting a thorough hiring process to ensure that you attract candidates who possess these qualities.

Jim Collins talks about this in his book *From Good to Great*. Just being good is not good enough. You want people who are enthusiastic and embrace your organization as their own. They understand how their role aligns with the goals of the business. In contrast, a bad culture fit is like a cancer; it eats away at morale and affects everyone.

This might mean you have to look beyond candidates' CVs in your hiring practices because a CV only tells part of the story. Anyone can give you a prepared answer to a standard set of interview questions. Make sure you evaluate potential employees in terms of culture: how they think, act, and respond to problems. Ask them about how they got interested in the role and what their career path looks like (and what they hope it will look like in the future). And don't be afraid to ask personal questions, as long as you're respectful. Ask about their life and what drives them.

Hire people with entrepreneurial drive. Hire people who enjoy what they do and seek to perform at a high level. Find someone who wants to stay with your company, values their contribution, and sees themselves as playing an essential role in the organization. Hiring the right people will save you time and money in the long run. Measure twice, cut once.

As an example of what happens when you hire people who aren't a good culture fit, while I was deployed in Afghanistan, I served under a colonel. He was an older gentleman, but he had never deployed before, which, as a colonel, is kind of a mark against him. That deployment for him was just a means to getting that patch on his arm; he wanted to tick all the boxes for his next promotion. In other words, his motives were wrong. And because of that, he wasn't willing to go the extra mile to complete the mission. He lacked leadership skills, was lazy, and very indecisive. And those characteristics—those failings of motive and skill—have real consequences, especially in the context of war, when lives are on the line.

For example, he would receive information but not disseminate it. And that gap in communication trickled down through the ranks. It quickly eroded everything the rest of us had worked so hard to build. Say an X-ray machine went down in Mazar-e-Sharif. He would hear that and not tell anyone, including me, the Health Information Systems Officer in charge of health communications across Afghanistan. He couldn't be bothered, even though it put patients' lives at risk and directly impacted the quality of their care. We wouldn't find out there was an urgent need until we heard it directly from the other Area of Operations that was having to chase us down. It made the rest of us, who were doing everything we could to support the mission, look bad, to say the least.

Breakdowns in leadership and communication like this can have a hugely negative impact on employee experience and morale. The people who *are* contributing will get frustrated because they feel like their ideas and efforts are falling on deaf ears or going unnoticed—or worse, they're being actively dismantled. As a leader, you must be willing to cut bait if you've hired the wrong person for the role.

Conversely, on my second deployment to Kuwait, my commanding officer was the operations officer, and he always had things on point. He knew exactly what we needed to do and communicated that. His leadership inspired everyone around him. Watching him, I thought, "This guy has his stuff together. I need to step my game up." Model positive behavior, and make sure leadership and management throughout your business do the same. You can put anyone on the field with someone like Tom Brady, and he will bring out the best in them, challenge them to be better, and make them look like Jerry Rice (ok, maybe not that good). For context, Jerry Rice is widely considered the greatest wide receiver in NFL history, known for his exceptional work ethic, skill, and consistent performance. When paired with a strong leader, even an average player could elevate their game—though becoming a legend like Rice is a high bar.

Having the right people in place will stimulate cohesion among your employees, boost morale, and improve employee experience. Beyond that, they will deliver better service to your clients, contribute ideas and energy to your business, and help build your brand. Moreover, there are material costs to recruiting, hiring, and training new employees. You don't want someone like the colonel, who is just using your business as a launching pad for the next thing. That will end up costing you in the long term, not to mention the negative impact it can have on your company culture and client experience in the meantime. So, be thorough and thoughtful when putting your team together. Think of it like a fantasy football team—you're assembling your dream team. You're going to pick Jerry Rice, not Jerry Garcia.

The elephant in the room with job satisfaction often comes down to simple material realities: pay and benefits. If you want to retain the talent you've worked so hard to attract, hire, and train, make sure you keep them on by continuing to offer them competitive pay for their effort and dedication. This might involve conducting regular salary reviews to ensure that your pay rates align with industry standards, offering comprehensive health and wellness benefits, and providing other perks and incentives such as flexible work arrangements, paid time off, or bonuses based on performance. Again, think of your fantasy football team—you have to pay the big bucks if you want to keep your star players from transferring to your rival's starting line-up.

Training Your Talent

Once you have hired the right employees, it is important to provide them with comprehensive training to ensure they are fully equipped to perform their duties. This goes beyond a couple of training videos and a few days of shadowing. Onboarding is an important step in the process when it comes to setting expectations for new employees, finding out what kind of support and training they need to succeed, and fostering alignment for your mission and values. Think of it like the honeymoon phase—this is where you establish the routines of your relationship. Make the most of this time!

A pivotal element of retaining top talent is providing them with opportunities for growth. Invest in employee development to improve their skills and knowledge. You want new employees to feel valued and guided, not just thrown to the wolves. This is especially true in the virtual world, where more businesses are offering remote or hybrid work options, which presents new challenges with onboarding, integration, and training. Employees can feel distant from their employers, managers, and colleagues. (You might notice the word "feel" popping up a lot throughout this book and in this chapter in particular. I cannot emphasize enough how important empathy is when it comes to your employees. How they feel is a key factor in their performance, so it's important for you to understand and respond appropriately to their feelings. You feel me?)

Investing in ongoing employee development ensures that your team members are continuously improving their skills and knowledge. This can involve providing access to training and development opportunities, offering mentorship programs, or even sponsoring employees to attend conferences or other relevant events. Mentoring—real mentoring—is a great way of strengthening the relationship between leadership and employees and transferring valuable skills. Real mentoring goes beyond surface-level guidance or one-off advice; it involves a committed, ongoing relationship where mentors actively invest in their mentees' growth, providing personalized feedback, fostering critical thinking, and facilitating skill development over time. This contrasts with what people commonly consider mentoring, which often implies occasional check-ins or generic advice lacking depth. Not only does your company benefit from upskilling employees through real mentoring, but it's also likely to boost their investment in and loyalty to your business. That said, again, it's important to keep training and development focused on specific goals or yardsticks. As practiced at most companies, especially small businesses, development is mostly ad hoc. A conference there, a seminar here, but there is no systematic plan. We need to be intentional about how we train and develop talent. To this end, create an individual development plan for every employee. Have that conversation within the first thirty days. Ask them about their career goals and what kind of training they're interested in. If someone tells you, "I don't want to be a manager; I just want to code for the rest of my life," let them! Ok, you can test them—let them take the lead on a project as an acting manager, but don't force it. For the most part, people will tell you where they want to be. It's your job to listen to them.

Another tactic is to experiment with job rotations. See what the right fit is for each employee. You want to retain your people, even if it means making adjustments. Strength is more than just what you're good at; it's also what you enjoy. Offer cross-training, not only for their current role but for others they might thrive in. That can germinate collaboration between people who don't normally work together, foster new areas of growth, and generate solutions for problem processes. You might even uncover someone's hidden passion or talent!

Lastly, you may want to consider stacking the deck when it comes to talent. If you find an outstanding candidate—someone with energy and experience—it can be wise to hire that person even if you don't have a role readily available. I often take the approach of, "Let's figure something out for you together." For instance, say a candidate interviewed for a software engineer role, but you think they are better suited as a solutions architect— have a conversation about exploring that option for them. My philosophy on training and development is to target the person, not the role. Show them you care and give them the autonomy they need to thrive.

Cultivating Culture

Look at *Fortune* or *Forbes'* lists of best companies to work for, and you will find the common thread is a strong focus on culture—the customs or norms of your workplace. One of your goals as a leader must be to create a culture that values teamwork, communication, and productivity. A positive work culture is essential for ensuring employees are happy, engaged, and motivated to perform their best work. This can involve fostering an environment of open communication, promoting teamwork and collaboration, recognizing and rewarding employee achievements, and providing opportunities for employees to have fun and socialize outside of work. Be inclusive and accommodating—people will have varied schedules and capacities—and you don't want to drive wedges between anyone.

Every company will be different. Even if you're a solopreneur, the culture of your company starts with you. Think about that as you set your mission and values and when you interact with customers, stakeholders, and third-party providers. It's your job to see the unseen and hear the unsaid as a leader. Authenticity is a key part of leadership, and that will be reflected in your culture.

As you might have gathered from some of the stories I've shared, I'm a big believer in learning through experience, growing from failure, and second chances. Because of that, my company's culture embraces freedom and autonomy, including the freedom to muck things up sometimes. No one likes to be micromanaged (and if they do—they were probably the wrong hire). Giving employees the autonomy they need to feel empowered does sometimes mean that they will fail. That's ok. Failure often leads to innovation. And freedom also leads to tenacity. We do what we need to get the job done. I always tell my employees, "Do things your way, and if you mess up, own it." We keep it real with each other. I want to challenge you to face failure and unearth the hidden gems buried in failure.

In the military, we use "after-action reports," or AARs, following any major incident. AARs are detailed summaries or critical analyses that examine what happened, how prepared we were, and what went well. Most importantly, they offer a plan of action to ensure we're better prepared for similar incidents in the future.

For example, we were attacked on base. The enemy came in through Gate 3. If Gates 1 and 2 had been attacked, what would have happened? Were there enough people on staff? Were they able to call in support? If you face failures or missteps in business, you can use AARs to respond and prepare for the future. Maybe you're missing your sales targets or have lost a big client. Tackle the problem as a team and work together to generate solutions. Remind employees that they aren't in this alone.

As we touched on earlier, another critical aspect of culture is creating meaningful work for people. Failing to do this is the number one mistake I see in a lot of small businesses. People want to be valued and challenged. They want to do something that matters. If you aren't providing your people with meaningful work, they will do the bare minimum to meet requirements, or they will start looking elsewhere for a company that will offer them meaning, value, and purpose. Now, you might think payroll or data entry can never be fulfilling—this is where your mission and values have to be rock solid. If you create a vision that your people want to get behind, everyone from the cleaners to the C-suite will feel a sense of satisfaction and accomplishment showing up to work.

Customers Count

Just as we looked at internal and external competition in the previous chapter, we need to look at people from both internal and external angles. Customers must be included in any successful people strategy. Just like you show your employees how much you value them—from hiring to training to retaining—you want your customers to know they are valued at every stage of the relationship. Many companies have great onboarding experiences for clients. They pull out all the stops to win the business, but after the client signs on, it's crickets. If you want to maintain a competitive edge, you have to consistently create value for your customers.

"Any fool can know. The point is to understand."
Albert Einstein hit the nail on the head when he said this. The first step to creating value for your customers is to understand their needs and expectations—and also know that these might change and evolve. To stay on top of the game, conduct customer surveys, analyze customer feedback, or speak directly with customers to gather insights into their preferences and pain points. And again, those pain points are just as important, especially if you're a service provider. Find out those weaknesses and how you can help address them. Usually, you will find that

their main issue has been staring them right in the face, and it wasn't until they failed enough that they felt like they needed to get help.

Back in 2022, I had the pleasure of working with a SaaS company, which we'll call Spectra Data Solutions, a rising tech startup specializing in data aggregation and analysis. They had a dynamic team and an innovative product but struggled with their business strategy. They knew that their data tools had potential but were unsure how to effectively cater to their customers' needs and expectations.

I was brought on board as a business consultant to help Spectra navigate this challenging landscape. My first order of business was to help them better understand their customers. To begin, we developed a comprehensive customer survey and reached out to current users of Spectra's platform and potential customers in their targeted industries. We gathered information about their customers' data analysis practices, their satisfaction with existing solutions, and, most importantly, areas where they felt their needs weren't being met.

The feedback was illuminating. Customers in the market were yearning for a more user-friendly interface, quicker data processing, and enhanced security measures. They were also interested in customized reports that could be tweaked according to their specific requirements. However, most of them found existing platforms, including Spectra's, lacking these features. This gap between customer expectations and existing market offerings meant Spectra had a significant opportunity.

I worked closely with their product development team, translating this valuable feedback into actionable changes to their product. The user interface was made more intuitive, a powerful data engine was incorporated for faster processing, security measures were bolstered, and a custom reporting module was added.

Following implementation, we communicated the upgrades to Spectra's clients, highlighting how the platform had been transformed based on *their* feedback. Not only did we see increased customer engagement and satisfaction, but there was also a significant rise in new customers, most of whom were referrals from satisfied users.

Understanding your customers' needs and expectations is the first and most crucial step to creating a positive customer experience. Spectra Data Solutions was able to use their customer insights to revolutionize their product, positioning themselves as a responsive and customer-centric brand in the market.

The Center of the Universe

You also want to develop a customer-centric approach to marketing and sales. Make their needs the focus of your efforts. This will look different for every company, depending on your USP. For example, you might aim to create personalized marketing campaigns that speak directly to your customers' needs and interests, offer exceptional customer service, or provide a seamless buying experience from start to finish.

Consider the lifetime value of a client to your business and then think of it from their perspective. What is their experience over that same lifetime? What happens when they become that customer? What is the value ladder? How do you make their experience with your business stand out against your competitors or their other service providers? Are they being heard and engaged with? Are their needs being met and their expectations exceeded? Are you making it fun for them to engage with you?

As a business coach, I've had the pleasure of working with a diverse range of companies, but one story that stands out is my work with ENDVR Active Community, a personal training company based in Houston, Texas. Before my arrival, ENDVR was already a well-regarded business, offering personalized training services to a broad array of clients. However, they faced challenges with stagnant growth and struggled to stand out in a competitive market. At the time, their marketing and sales strategies were largely product-centric. They had a wide range of excellent personal training packages, but the company was more focused on selling these packages without necessarily considering the unique needs and preferences of their clients.

The solution was to shift from a product-centric approach to a customer-centric one—a significant strategic change for ENDVR, a community gym. Through client surveys, focus groups, and data analysis, we gained a clear understanding of their clients, who fell into three main categories: fitness enthusiasts looking for advanced training programs, busy professionals seeking quick and effective workouts, and families interested in inclusive, community-oriented fitness solutions. With this data, we segmented the customer base accordingly and crafted targeted marketing efforts for each group.

For the fitness enthusiasts, we highlighted ENDVR's advanced training packages, showcasing specialized classes, personal coaching sessions, and performance tracking tools. For busy professionals, we emphasized the convenience of flexible scheduling, express workout programs, and mobile app accessibility to fit workouts seamlessly into their schedules. For families, we promoted family-friendly classes and community events that fostered a welcoming atmosphere. With these tailored marketing campaigns, we created personalized messages that resonated with each segment, enhancing engagement and membership growth.

Additionally, we offered customized training packages where clients could select services that matched their needs, whether group classes, one-on-one training, or on-demand video sessions. To further improve the customer experience, we provided detailed information about each service on the website, simplified the membership sign-up process, and ensured customer support was easily accessible to address any inquiries or issues.

We didn't stop at the sale either. We made sure to follow up with customers to get their feedback and ensure they were satisfied with their purchases. This improved customer satisfaction and led to valuable insights that we used to refine their offerings further.

The transformation of ENDVR Active Community has been dramatic. Since implementing the customer-centric approach, they have experienced significant growth in their client base and a dramatic increase in customer loyalty and satisfaction. By focusing on the needs and preferences of their customers,

ENDVR was able to stand out in a crowded market and establish a strong reputation for being a customer-focused personal training company. The clients appreciated the personalized approach and felt they were truly part of a community, leading to higher retention rates and more word-of-mouth referrals. The success story of ENDVR Active Community is a testament to the power of a customer-centric approach to marketing and sales.

A key aspect of this was a transformation of the customer experience at every stage in the relationship—from buying the service to usability to customer support down the line. And remember, your customers are also an extension of your culture. You want them to feel involved in, loyal to, and motivated by your mission and values. You want them rocking your star player's jersey and supporting the home team. Keep that in mind as you build on those relationships. You want customers to grow with you—not outgrow you.

Data Drives Everything

Monitoring customer feedback and tracking key metrics such as customer satisfaction and Net Promoter Score (NPS) is important to ensure you deliver only the best. Based on these insights, you can identify areas for improvement and make changes to your approach to better meet the needs and expectations of your customers.

In the sweltering heat of summer 2023, I was brought in as a business consultant to collaborate with US Power Pros, a small but ambitious company based in Houston, Texas (you might remember our friend the electrician entrepreneur from the last chapter). Their main line of business was electrician services, and they had recently added Generac power generators to their product line. They aspired to become the top Generac supplier in the region, but they were struggling with a slew of challenges that included dwindling customer satisfaction, an onslaught of negative Google reviews, and poor brand visibility.

When I first met Tad, the owner, his face was sunken with stress, and his eyes dimmed by the desperation he felt for his business. He had worked tirelessly to build his company from the ground up, and it pained him to see it floundering.

Our initial assessment revealed the core of their issues to be the lack of a customer-centric approach. It was clear that Tad and his team were extremely knowledgeable about their products but lacked the know-how to make their customer service as stellar as their technical expertise. Our first order of business was to implement a robust system to collect and monitor customer feedback. We started by refining their Google My Business profile and encouraging happy customers to leave reviews. Additionally, we utilized an automated email system to collect Net Promoter Scores (NPS) after each service or installation. We were transparent with customers, explaining that their feedback was crucial for our improvement.

Within a few weeks, we began to notice patterns. Customers wanted quicker response times and clearer communication about the services they were receiving, and they felt that the technicians could be friendlier. Armed with this knowledge, we worked with Tad and his team to address these issues. We trained the staff in customer service soft skills, teaching them how to communicate effectively with clients and convey a sense of friendliness and empathy even under pressure. We also implemented a new ticketing system that included a chatbot and guaranteed a response to any customer query within twenty-four hours.

Over the next few months, customer satisfaction soared, and negative Google reviews decreased significantly. The positive impact on the company's image led to an uptick in sales inquiries for Generac power generators. US Power Pros was finally on the path to becoming the top Generac supplier in the region. Tad, once fraught with worry, now wore a smile of satisfaction. With its humble Houston roots, US Power Pros has become a prime example of why good data on customer feedback should be at the heart of every business strategy.

The Rest of the Story

That first night in jail, I got on my knees in that freezing cold cell and prayed to God. It was the first time in my life I prayed of my own volition. I said it in my own words, asking for strength, a chance to make things right, and guidance to find a new path forward. I pleaded, "God, if You give me a way out of this, I promise I will change. Show me what I need to do.

And that night, I dreamt I was free. I dreamt I was happy. I felt light. My family and I were on vacation somewhere. We were laughing. Through the floor-to-ceiling window, I looked out to the crystal blue waters of the ocean. It was beautiful. I felt like I was seeing an alternate path unfold before me if I could just hold onto that dream. Prior to my brush with the law, I had been drifting along. I was that boat without a destination. School came easily for me, but I treated it like a joke. I would roll dice with my friends, get my hair braided, and go to lunch for three periods of the day. People always told me, "You need to go to school so you can get a good job." But everyone around me was poor, so the idea of "getting a good job" never resonated. I didn't know anyone who had a good job! So then, what was the point of going to school?

But the incident changed me. I got more serious. Seeing the pain my choices had caused my mom, and the weariness I saw on my sisters' faces when they visited me in jail made me think twice. And I also finally saw how much they cared about me. I thought harder about what I was doing. Facing seven years in prison—it humbled me. For the first time, I reevaluated my path.

I remember one guy who was on the floor with me. He and his twin brother were part of the Crips. He was the driver in a robbery that went bad. He was charged with the murder that went down in the course of events, even though he wasn't the gunman. I felt for him because, like me, he hadn't even left the car—he had no idea what was going down.

A couple of weeks later, I was released. When I left, that guy from my floor said, "I'll see you when I get out." But I knew I'd never see him again. I made myself a promise to cut all ties with anyone and anything that might lead me back to that jail cell. I had finally realized that life had more to offer. That I had more to offer. I began to change the narrative. It wasn't immediate, but it was a start—to redefine my life, navigate away from the path of theft, and find a way to escape not just poverty but also the mentality that being born poor meant you had to stay that way. It was a painful and difficult journey filled with regrets and harsh lessons, but also one of growth and self-discovery. It's how I moved from a life defined by desperation to a life driven by determination.

As a leader, it is important to remember that you're not the only one impacted by your decisions and actions. You have to learn to go with your gut. When I was in that car, I had a gut feeling the night would end badly. I ignored my gut, and it landed me in jail. I should have spoken up. I should have told them to stop; I should have extricated myself from the situation right away. In the military, we say that as the leader, you must be willing to live with the consequences.

As it turned out, my friend Dave had snitched and pinned it on the three of us. He has to live with that. I got six months' probation. And I learned from that experience and moved on. Meanwhile, my best friend Rese told everyone that I was sick and that's why I hadn't been in school. The day I came back, I told everyone, "Yeah, man, I'm good. I feel much better now." It was the truth. I felt a lot better being at school than in jail!

NOTES

CHAPTER 4: TECHNOLOGY

Now, let's look at the next critical factor: technology. Although I've shifted into coaching, I'm still a geek at heart. I love technology—and it's one area I find many clients need a lot of help with. When I joined the military, I scored high on the Armed Services Vocational Aptitude Battery (ASVAB), and the recruiter said that I could choose any military occupational specialty (MOS) I wanted. My top choices were military intelligence and IT—I chose IT. IT was a rapidly expanding field and a skillset I thought would be transferrable down the line.

I quickly learned the importance of having the right systems in tech. I did everything from working the help desk and resolving mundane everyday issues ("Sir, have you tried turning the computer off and then on again?") to being the health information systems officer and maintaining critical health systems all over Afghanistan—slightly higher stakes than the old help desk. My first job after leaving the military was at the Pentagon at the Network Operations and Security Center. I worked in Windows administration and security—patching updates, maintaining the firewall, and administering user group management. That's all to say: I live for this stuff.

There's such a broad range of tools and tech out there that many entrepreneurs and business owners don't know what they need. How do you know what technology best fits the needs of your company, your employees, and your clients? Again, "yield" is all about identifying the *right* levers to pull to achieve your goals (your "yardstick") and find success. In this chapter, we'll talk in-depth about the core tech that each service-based business needs—and why you need it, even if you think you don't!

Before we get into it, let me set your mind at ease. Many business owners I've worked with feel overwhelmed at the first mention of technology. Maybe you think your business is running just fine the old-school way. Or maybe you don't think you have the budget for a big tech overhaul. I'm here to tell you that implementing new technology doesn't have to be as hard—or costly—as you think. You don't have to know everything; you just need to know enough to understand how it works. Think of technology as a force multiplier, not a hindrance. Let it do the heavy lifting. Its purpose is to make your life—and your employees' lives—easier.

Tech Solutions for Efficiency and Productivity

The most significant advantages of having the right technology are efficiency and productivity. Streamlining processes like data collection and analysis can save your business time, money, and stress. So, the first step is to evaluate your current technology, find the gaps and opportunities for better systems, and implement technology solutions that improve efficiency and productivity.

Conduct a thorough assessment of your business processes and identify areas where technology can be used to increase efficiency and productivity. This could include implementing project management software, using cloud-based storage solutions, or investing in customer relationship management (CRM) systems. Evaluate different technology solutions based on their functionality, cost, and compatibility with your existing systems before deciding which to implement. At the end of the chapter, I'll walk you through the four core technologies every service-based business should have as part of its technology strategy. But first, I'll share a story about why having the *right* technology for your business is so important.

Simplify, Simplify, Simplify: A Case Study

"Our life is frittered away by detail. Simplify, simplify, simplify! I say, let your affairs be as two or three, and not a hundred or a thousand; instead of a million count half a dozen, and keep your accounts on your thumb-nail," wrote Henry David Thoreau in *Walden*. Now, I'm not suggesting we all swan off to a cabin on a lake and become hermits, but my man here has a point. Many of us spend our working lives exhausted with endless to-do lists. We take on too much, bite off more than we can chew, especially as business owners and entrepreneurs. Thankfully, the world of technology has grown leaps and bounds since Thoreau's day, and there are fantastic options to help you get that to-do list to fit on the proverbial thumbnail.

This is where Bruno comes into the story. I began coaching Bruno, a digital marketer based in Portugal, after he came to me for help with lead generation. His business, I quickly realized, suffered from having too much technology. Excited by the prospect of all the cool new tools, Bruno had built a bulky, unwieldy technology strategy. He had six systems, all performing the same essential function. He held a summit on Bigmarker that served as his primary driver for lead generation, but he also had a WordPress site, ClickFunnels for an affiliate program, ThriveCart (another platform for creating funnels and cart pages for businesses), and a few more systems on top of that! In other words, he was spending money on a whole host of technology for just one lead magnet. It was costly, and it was more than he could manage—not exactly a winning combination.

To make matters worse, he needed a plugin for his WordPress, but when that broke, he didn't know how to fix it. Suddenly, all his links were broken, too. Not to mention, the expense of all those systems was starting to add up and overwhelm his budget.

The solution was simple, literally. He needed to simplify. Everything he was doing could be done on one platform. We moved everything to his WordPress site. We used WordPress plugins, scrapped unnecessary technology, and made it more native. The finished product was seamless. Changing platforms also allowed them to upgrade their user experience. Now, it was streamlined, elegant, and cohesive. Customers could access everything they needed in one place. In the end, he saved thousands of dollars (well, Euros) on technology expenses while simultaneously boosting his sales figures. Sometimes, simple is better. It all comes down to what serves your goals and works best for your business.

Use It or Lose It

It's not enough to simply purchase and set up a technology system—you have to *use* it. You have to learn to make it work for you. For instance, look to data analytics to gain insights into your business operations and identify areas where technology can drive improvements. Data analytics can help you locate bottlenecks in your processes or determine which areas of your business are most profitable. This data can help inform decisions about which technology solutions to invest in and how to prioritize technology projects.

I hear disaster stories all the time. One common mistake is buying a technology product and not setting it up properly. Take CRMs, for example: if you aren't tracking where people are in the pipeline, then what's the point? You might have a call scheduled with a client, but if you haven't tracked their journey with you, you might not even know what that call is meant to be about! If you don't have a way to tag people in your CRM based on how they discovered you, that's a mistake.

The beauty of a CRM is that it allows for customization and personalization at every level. That means your marketing and client touches can—and should—be meaningful and useful to prospects and clients. You need to know who is opening what links. Who reads every one of your emails? Tag that person as a hot lead! Which campaigns worked and which ones didn't?

And don't be afraid to test things yourself. If you don't want a full-blown CRM, try an EMM (email marketing management) tool. Use the tools that fit your business. That might mean opting for the smaller or lesser-known technology. And there are a range of free options that do the job just fine. I'm a big fan of getting technology and solutions from AppSumo because it's cheaper, and you can land lifetime deals—ever heard of Shopify or Zapier? Don't make it complicated, and don't feel intimidated by jargon.

The other important factor in making technology work for your business is monitoring and updating technology solutions to ensure they remain effective. Technology solutions are not a one-time investment; they require ongoing maintenance and updates. Monitor the performance of your technology solutions and regularly review their effectiveness. Update your technology solutions as needed to ensure they continue to meet your needs and remain compatible with other systems across your business.

Automation = Acceleration (and the End of Aggravation)

Automation tools can be used to streamline repetitive tasks, reduce errors, and increase efficiency. This could include automating tasks such as data entry, scheduling, or customer follow-ups. Look for automation tools that integrate with your existing systems and can be customized to meet your needs. We'll look at specific tools and how to integrate them into your business in depth later in the chapter, but it's important to include an overview here as part of your big-picture technology strategy. For now, I'll share another story to illustrate just how great an impact automation can have when implemented with intention.

If You Build It, They Will Come

A young, energetic coach, Cindy, sought me out after launching her coaching business. She was recently divorced and had three kids. She had quit her job in the medical field and put everything on the line to start her new business. Five months in, she was struggling to get off the ground. She hadn't managed to recruit any clients.

"I quit my job to invest in this. Coaching is my calling, but I don't know what I'm doing. I don't even know how to get leads to attract clients," she said.

We started with the basics. I helped her implement a system to automate lead generation. We created two lead magnets to test (A/B testing). One was a downloadable eBook on overcoming overwhelm, the idea for which was based on a survey of her two hundred followers regarding what kind of content they'd like to read. Then, we created a 45-minute, evergreen webinar with Cindy speaking on confidence. So, we established our two funnels. (I always advise clients to start with a low-touch strategy, like an eBook, in conjunction with a high-touch strategy, like a webinar where people can ask questions and interact directly.)

For prospects to access these materials, they had to provide their email addresses. Then, once they signed up for the email, we hit them up with the welcome sequence of five emails, giving them even more exposure to her brand, ideas, and coaching. For Cindy, it was a means to get inbound leads, which meant she didn't have to do all the chasing. All she had to do was put the links in her bios on social media and professional websites, and the leads came pouring in. And because this step was automated,

Cindy could follow up with prospects on the next step even when she was busy!

After reading the eBook or watching the webinar, prospects were invited to the next step on the value ladder. For instance, on the webinar, there was a popup that said, "If you're ready to build confidence, click this link." That took them to a sales page where they could schedule a call and sign up for coaching sessions, along with other paid options for continuing contact and accessing more materials.

Moreover, which lead magnet prospects chose—either the eBook or the webinar—gave Cindy an indication of what content they were looking for when they scheduled a call. From that, she knew what they wanted and could tailor what she said to persuade them to work with her. Down the line, we used this same type of funnel to set up a group coaching service.

Cindy has since been able to generate $20,000 per month just by implementing a few simple technologies.

The primary advantage of automation is that it puts out that big welcome sign to prospects and clients. So, let the technology roll out the red carpet on your behalf.

The Core Four

I recommend four main technology systems to nearly all my clients. Think of them like the four legs of a table—you need all four to be equally sturdy and stable. These are big umbrella categories, so the precise way you implement and use them might differ, but the need for them will always be the same. The "core four" that every business needs are a scheduling tool, a prospecting tool, analytics, and a customer relationship management (CRM) system. Let's look at each of these and discuss why they matter and how you can make them work for your business.

Scheduling Tools

Time is not just money; it's the core around which everything revolves. Ensuring that appointments, meetings, and tasks are organized effectively is paramount to success. This is where scheduling tools come into play. Scheduling tools are essential, and using them effectively can enhance your business' productivity and client satisfaction.

Automated Appointments. Without an automated system, scheduling can become a chaotic and time-consuming process. A scheduling tool allows clients to book their appointments at their convenience, reducing back-and-forth communication and eliminating human errors.

Integrated Calendars. Synchronizing your appointments with your existing calendars ensures everything is in one place. It minimizes the risk of double bookings and helps keep track of all appointments and events.

Customization and Flexibility. Most scheduling tools provide customization options, allowing you to set working hours, break times, and even special days. This flexibility ensures that your schedule reflects your actual availability.

Enhanced Client Engagement. With features like automated reminders and confirmation emails, scheduling tools enhance client engagement. They reduce no-shows and provide clients with a professional and convenient booking experience.

A scheduling tool is not just a convenience; it's a vital asset for any service-based business. It brings efficiency, professionalism, and a level of control that manual scheduling simply cannot provide.

Prospecting Tools

Prospecting tools are designed to simplify and enhance the often tedious, trial-and-error process of acquiring new clients. These tools offer an array of features to identify and reach potential clients in a targeted, efficient way.

Streamlining Lead Generation. Manual prospecting can be a cumbersome and time-consuming process. Prospecting tools automate this task, allowing businesses to generate leads from various channels without investing countless hours.

Enhanced Targeting and Segmentation. Service-based businesses often need to reach specific demographics. Prospecting tools enable businesses to categorize prospects based on certain criteria, allowing for more targeted and effective outreach.

Data-driven Insights. Understanding how prospects engage with your content and respond to your outreach efforts can provide invaluable insights. Prospecting tools offer analytics that help in refining strategies to improve results.

Integrating with Marketing and Sales Efforts. Prospecting doesn't exist in isolation; it's part of the overall marketing and sales funnel. Prospecting tools integrate seamlessly with other platforms, ensuring a cohesive approach to client acquisition.

Analytics (e.g., Google Analytics)

Google Analytics is the first tech you should install on your site. It's free and powerful. It gives you rich data and insights—far too many to list here. But let me assure you, if you don't set that up, you are missing out. Without proper data, you won't last long. You won't know what's happening in your business, and you won't be able to *anticipate* shifts, changes, or trends. You'll be doing everything ad hoc. When it comes to business strategy, you want to be active, not reactive; analytics are one of the best tools to help you do that. Here are just a few of the ways your business can benefit.

Understanding Customer Behavior. Analytics tools allow you to track and analyze how customers interact with your website or app. Understanding these patterns can lead to more personalized services and targeted marketing strategies.

Performance Tracking. Whether it's a marketing campaign, a product launch, or a new service offering, analytics tools gauge the performance of various business initiatives, helping you recognize what works and where improvements are needed.

Optimizing Conversions. Converting visitors into customers is vital for business growth. Analytics tools provide insights into conversion rates and identify the bottlenecks and opportunities to enhance conversion paths.

Data-Driven Decision Making. Intuition and experience are valuable, but supplementing them with hard data leads to more reliable and effective decisions. Analytics tools provide this data, turning guesswork into strategic planning.

Real-Time Insights. Real-time data can make a significant difference. Analytics tools provide up-to-the-minute information, enabling you to respond quickly to emerging trends or issues.

Cost Efficiency. Understanding where your efforts are bearing fruit and where they are falling short allows you to allocate resources more efficiently. Analytics tools enable this understanding, leading to cost-saving decisions.

CRMs

Customer relationship management tools (CRMs) are a one-stop shop for, well, managing customer relationships. They can show you the entire life cycle of a client relationship and provide invaluable data for decision-making and insights on retaining your customers.

Centralized Customer Information. A CRM system consolidates all customer information in one place. This includes contact details, purchase history, preferences, and interactions. This centralized repository ensures that every team member has access to the same, consistent information, enhancing collaboration and understanding.

Improved Customer Engagement. With a CRM, personalized communication becomes easier and more efficient. Understanding the customer's history and preferences enables more targeted and relevant interactions, thus enhancing engagement and satisfaction.

Streamlined Sales Process. A CRM system tracks every stage of the sales process, from lead generation to conversion. It allows sales teams to manage pipelines effectively, prioritize efforts, and close deals more efficiently.

Enhanced Customer Support. Customer support is critical in service-based businesses. CRM systems facilitate faster response times and more personalized support by providing all necessary customer information at the fingertips of support staff.

Marketing Automation Integration. CRM systems can be integrated with marketing tools to create targeted campaigns based on customer behavior and segmentation. This leads to more effective marketing efforts and higher conversion rates.

Data-Driven Insights. *Through reporting and analytics,* CRM systems offer insights into customer behavior, sales trends, and overall business performance. These insights guide strategic decision-making and continuous improvement.

Every business has its own needs. You'll have your own goals and a unique selling prospect, which means the exact technology tools you need will also be different.

NOTES

CHAPTER 5: PERSONAL SWOT ANALYSIS

AS YOU CONSIDER THE LEVERS AT YOUR DISPOSAL TO HELP ACHIEVE YOUR GOALS, ONE tool I return to time again with clients is the personal SWOT analysis. In the ever-evolving world of leadership development, identifying and leveraging effective strategies is crucial. While many tools and frameworks exist to facilitate this growth, one business strategy stands out for its versatility and comprehensive approach: the SWOT analysis. Originally designed to assess organizational strategy, the SWOT analysis—examining strengths, weaknesses, opportunities, and threats—offers an equally powerful framework for personal growth and leadership development.

I use SWOT analysis constantly in business, and one day, I thought, why don't I do this for myself? In this version, the traditional SWOT analysis for leadership development turns the mirror on the leader himself. That means it's taken from your perspective to see what you're good at and what lights you up. What do you love doing? Maybe you love mentoring others, building new strategies from the ground up, or diving deep into data analysis to find trends. Maybe you're at your best when leading a team through complex challenges or creating innovative solutions that push your business forward. In any event, this personal SWOT analysis allows for more granular self-analysis. It helps you pinpoint your strengths and passions so you can lean into them more effectively and align your leadership approach with what drives you. It also forces you to confront your weaknesses, consider employee feedback, and really dig deep into the question of "What can I do better?" We touched on the idea of a personal SWOT analysis in Chapter 1 in our discussion of goal setting; now, we're going to go all in.

First off, let's address why this is so important. There is no doubt you worked your butt off to get where you are. Maybe your employees all think you're the best boss ever, and you have clients lining up to sign with you. Still, we all have opportunities to improve, face situations head-on, improve our skills, or break new ground. Even Michael Jordan, one of the greatest athletes of all time, acknowledged the need to consistently put in effort to stay at the top: "The game has its ups and downs, but you can never lose focus of your individual goals, and you can't let yourself be beat because of lack of effort."

His may be *very* big shoes to fill, but the least we can do is try. So, ask yourself, where have I fallen short? What are my blind spots? Take the time to sit down and consider everything you don't normally think about. Maybe you've struggled with effective communication during high-pressure situations or overlooked the importance of delegating tasks to your team. Perhaps you tend to avoid feedback because it feels uncomfortable. And the more you apply this practice—and you can do it over and over again throughout your career—the more you will improve in the long term. Using the SWOT analysis as a tool for personal, professional, and leadership development sets a shining example for your team, as well. Have your employees do this for themselves so they can identify areas of growth and opportunity. Or use it as a feedback tool. Have your employees—by team, department, or as a whole, including the management team—conduct SWOT analyses (anonymously, of course). Then, study the results. Are there recurring themes? Where does the feedback overlap? You'll get a more layered, nuanced picture of the whole landscape of your business and your staff. So, what's the best place to start?

Start with Your Strengths

First, it's essential to recognize the attributes that make us effective leaders. What are the unique qualities and capabilities that allow you to excel and set you apart? In the realm of leadership, your strengths may range from strategic thinking and effective communication to empathy and problem-solving. During turbulent times, these strengths serve as your beacon, guiding you safely through the storm. They provide a foundation upon which you can lean and navigate through the uncertainties and challenges inherent in leadership roles. Moreover, you can leverage these strengths to your advantage. Use them to inspire, motivate, and lead.

When I first applied the question of strengths to myself as a leader, I recognized that I was empathetic, good at connecting with people, and enabled people to feel safe sharing with me. I'm a strong communicator. I can convey complex topics in a distilled way, and people enjoy talking to me because I'm charismatic.

These are valuable qualities in a leader that have made it possible for me to serve a wide range of clients.

Identify Weaknesses

Once more, Michael Jordan has some words of wisdom for us and the subject at hand. He said, "My attitude is that if you push me toward something that you think is a weakness, then I will turn that perceived weakness into a strength." Recognizing your strengths is only one piece of the SWOT puzzle. Identifying your weaknesses is equally important.

It's easy to view weaknesses as personal inadequacies, but weaknesses take on a new significance within the context of leadership development. They become opportunities for growth and learning, areas for improvement that can strengthen your leadership capabilities. Embracing weaknesses promotes self-awareness and encourages a deeper understanding of ourselves as leaders. By seeking to improve in these areas, we set ourselves on a path of continuous personal and leadership development.

When I started my career as a business coach, I was no Jordan. I had just gotten "off the bench," so to speak, and into the game. I had a lot to learn. My biggest weakness was that I wasn't good at pitching my services. And you won't get far in business if you can't sell yourself. I'm a great communicator, but I had to learn to tailor that to my new industry and the clients I wanted to attract. I had to learn the art of the pitch.

I also had to learn what resources I had at my disposal and how to acquire those resources. You don't know what you don't know. I didn't know how to network. I needed to develop the skills that would put me in the orbit of thought leaders and key players. That led me to establishing powerful relationships with the right people.

Finally, I was doing the "heart work," but I often avoided the sensitive subject of money with clients. I didn't know how to broach the subject of pricing. I undercharged for my services. I avoided the business side of things. I wasn't yet comfortable valuing myself to clients how I knew I should. I was too empathetic. One of the things I love about my work is the opportunity to serve others, but at the same time, I had to acknowledge that I needed to serve myself, too.

Take Advantage of Opportunities

In the journey toward becoming a better leader, opportunities will arise that can help you progress and grow. Despite their potential benefits, it can be all too easy to overlook these opportunities amidst the hustle and bustle of life. Nonetheless, it is crucial that you seize these opportunities, no matter how small, as they can act as sparks of hope illuminating your path toward even more significant goals. Common opportunities that leaders encounter include taking on challenging new projects that push them out of their comfort zones, learning new skills to stay ahead in their field, expanding networks to foster valuable connections, and accepting mentorship that provides guidance and wisdom. These opportunities open doors to new dimensions of personal and leadership growth and can set the stage for transformative development.

When I started coaching, I sought out the opportunity to work on these weaknesses. The best way for me to do that was to hire someone better at selling and closing and someone to set appointments with my growing network of key players. We'll discuss delegation at length later in the book, but this was a key opportunity for my own growth. I also hired a mentor (yes, coaches have coaches!) who knew the coaching business. Their tutelage was key to my personal and professional development, and I was also able to leverage their network to my advantage.

Pay Attention to Threats

The final piece of the SWOT analysis is threats. These represent challenges or obstacles that could hinder your growth or performance. At first glance, threats might seem disheartening, even overwhelming. However, if you can adopt a growth-oriented mindset, you will see that these threats are, in fact, challenges in disguise. They will test your resilience, but they also offer the chance to confront them, battle them, and ultimately emerge stronger. These challenges or threats can catalyze transformation, pushing you out of your comfort zone and promoting personal growth and enhanced leadership skills.

My relative newness on the scene read to some as inexperience, and that was a threat. Coaches with more experience and better brand visibility were snatching away my clients. Another threat was the size of my company. I was and still am a solopreneur. Bigger organizations I wanted to partner with may have dismissed me because of the size of my business. Clients might see that as an inability to deliver the required services and think they need to recruit a larger coaching firm. (They would be wrong—and the proof is in the pudding.) Lastly, as a small business, I don't have an endless marketing budget, a staff of hundreds, or limitless time. This threatened the sustainability and scalability of BrightMind Consulting Group.

Threats may be viewed as "future potential problems," but the problems of tomorrow emerge from the oversights of today. It's important to be aware of these threats and develop the means to address them. You don't have to look particularly far down the road. I tend to think long-term, but usually, I try to limit my analyses to three years. The business landscape changes so much that it's hard to predict beyond that in a meaningful way.

Better Leadership Through Reflection

Incorporating the SWOT analysis into our leadership development strategy equips us with a comprehensive, structured, and insightful tool for self-assessment and growth. It empowers us to see ourselves clearly, acknowledging our strengths and weaknesses. It reminds us to stay alert for opportunities and teaches us to face our threats head-on, using them as catalysts for growth. In doing so, we not only survive our leadership journey—we thrive. By understanding our strengths and weaknesses, seizing opportunities, and bravely facing threats, we can foster our growth as leaders.

I'm serious when I say I use the SWOT analysis all the time for myself and my business. For example, I used the SWOT analysis when I rebranded from Live Not Loathe to BrightMind Consulting Group. I realized Live Not Loathe was antiquated; it didn't connote consulting or business services. I was virtually invisible on Google. That was a weakness and a threat.

Since the rebrand, BrightMind Consulting Group shows up high in Google searches for consultants. It's better for keyword searches and SEO. As a result, I'm getting more inquiries from the kind of people I want to work with, and prospects know what I'm about before they even come to me. There's no ambiguity. I occupy a unique space where personal development and business development meet. It's the kind of brand name and recognition—because I am the brand—that lends itself to long-term sustainability and scalability. People who find me on LinkedIn know right away what I provide.

But don't just take my word for it. You know I love a story, so let's widen the scope a little. Let's look at what happens, start to finish, when you utilize and apply this powerful tool.

SWOT Meets IT

I worked with a client, Shelton, who had recently opened an IT shop in a rural town in North Carolina. He had never run his own business before and brought me on as a coach to help him find his feet. Of course, I helped him do a personal SWOT analysis so we could set goals and determine a course of action for achieving those goals.

Shelton had a lot going for him. He had a lot of strengths. First and foremost, he had technical acumen. He knew his stuff, whether it was phones, laptops, desktops—whatever it was, he could fix it, and he knew everything there was to know about the tech spec on it. He was deeply invested and rooted in his community. As a locally oriented business, this was essential. He had a solid network from which to build. And he was personable, which meant he was well-liked by his neighbors and customers. He was also skilled in problem-solving, adaptability, and communication. He could quickly find solutions to complex problems, was accustomed to the fast-paced changes of the tech world, and was great at translating technical jargon into comprehensible language for his clients.

Still, like all of us, he had his weaknesses. He lacked experience in the field. Although he was personable, he wasn't inclined to introduce himself because he was somewhat shy. That meant he was not particularly good at networking. On top of that, he also had a full-time day job, so the hours he had available to invest in his own business were limited. He struggled with work-life balance, which strained his relationship with his two boys and led to burnout. This, in part, was also related to his weakness when it came to delegation. Shelton found it hard to let go of specific tasks, which led to inefficiency and stress. Lastly, though he knew the tech world well, he needed to broaden his business acumen and develop marketing, finance, and human resources skills.

Being a relatively new business owner, Shelton had lots of opportunities for growth. He could upskill himself by attaining professional certifications to boost his credibility. Networking was another area of leadership development. He had to build his own confidence if he was going to take advantage of all the opportunities there are in the IT world to connect with like-minded professionals, from conferences to online forums.

There were plenty of opportunities on the business side as well, but these were Shelton's main areas of personal and leadership development.

There were also real threats. Other, more established competitors in his field had good reputations in the community. The competitive landscape had the potential to lead to exhaustion, discouragement, and inaction. His ability to grow and expand was threatened by his other job and limitations on his time. The fast pace of technological changes can also be a drain on your schedule if you want to keep pace and stay in the loop. Time management became an essential skill for Shelton to hone.

With this SWOT analysis, Shelton was able to take stock of the big picture. He felt reassured in his abilities and knowledge, and we aimed for him to leverage his technical acumen and problem-solving skills to establish best practices across his business. We also developed a plan to address those weaknesses and threats. For example, I encouraged Shelton to engage in leadership and management training courses focused on improving communication and delegation skills. I also suggested that he consider hiring or consulting experts in business areas where he needed more depth and to develop a robust risk management plan that monitors market trends and competition. In this way, he was able to turn threats into opportunities.

Sample SWOT Analysis

To craft your personal SWOT analysis, begin by quickly listing your top several strengths, weaknesses, opportunities, and threats in quadrants, as in the example below. Then put more thought into each one to provide yourself a reference later on.

STRENGTHS	WEAKNESSES
- Unique Expertise - Personal Connection - Proven Frameworks - Flexibility - Word-of-Mouth Marketing	- Limited Time and Resources - Over-Dependence on a Few Clients - Fear of Delegation - Lack of Metrics
OPPORTUNITIES	THREATS
- Scaling Services - Leveraging the Book - Expanding Marketing Efforts - Networking - Growing Demand for Expertise	- Market Saturation - Economic Downturns - Burnout - Rapidly Changing Trends - Technology Disruption

Strengths

- *Unique Expertise:* I have specialized knowledge and skills in my service area (e.g., coaching, consulting, design, etc.), which differentiate me from competitors.
- *Personal Connection:* My ability to connect emotionally with clients builds trust and loyalty.

- *Proven Frameworks:* I've developed systems and processes (like the 5Y Framework) that consistently deliver results for clients.
- *Flexibility:* Being a small business owner allows me to quickly adapt to client needs and market trends.
- *Word-of-Mouth Marketing:* Happy clients regularly refer me to others, providing organic growth.

Weaknesses

- *Limited Time and Resources:* I often wear multiple hats, which can dilute my focus and prevent me from scaling effectively.
- *Inconsistent Marketing:* My marketing efforts are sporadic, often relying on word of mouth rather than a strategic plan.
- *Over-Dependence on a Few Clients:* A large percentage of my revenue comes from a small client base, increasing financial vulnerability.
- *Fear of Delegation:* I struggle to let go of tasks, which prevents me from focusing on high-level growth strategies.
- *Lack of Metrics:* I don't always track KPIs, making it hard to measure progress and optimize my strategies.

Opportunities

- *Scaling Services:* By creating digital products (e.g., courses, templates, or guides), I can generate passive income and serve more clients without additional time investment.
- *Leveraging the Book:* The book can position me as a thought leader in my industry, opening doors for speaking engagements, partnerships, and higher-paying clients.

- *Expanding Marketing Efforts:* Consistent social media, email campaigns, and content marketing can help me reach a broader audience.
- *Networking:* Attending industry conferences and events can lead to valuable collaborations and new client opportunities.
- *Growing Demand for Expertise:* With businesses increasingly focused on leadership and transformation, there is a growing market for my services.

Threats

- *Market Saturation:* The rise in competition from other service-based entrepreneurs could make it harder to stand out.
- *Economic Downturns:* Tight budgets during economic challenges might lead clients to cut back on non-essential services.
- *Burnout:* The risk of overworking myself without proper delegation or systems could negatively impact my health and business.
- *Rapidly Changing Trends:* Industry trends and client expectations are constantly evolving, requiring me to stay ahead of the curve.
- *Technology Disruption:* Advances in AI and automation could replace certain services or reduce their perceived value.

Remember, leadership development is a journey, and the SWOT analysis is a compass that can guide us in the right direction. In a conversation with Alan Weiss, the million-dollar consultant, on my podcast, *Design Your Life and Business*, he told me, "Life is not about a search for meaning but the creation of meaning."[1] That creation of meaning can be both personal and professional. So, let's embark on this journey of self-discovery, growth, and transformation to become the leaders we aspire to be. In the next chapter, we'll look at the next piece of the 5Y Framework—yare—and how to make that journey smooth and easy.

Section Summary:

- Achieving goals requires a focused strategy and resource allocation.

- Efficiency and consistency are key to maximizing yield in your business efforts.

- Align your team's strengths with the goals to ensure smooth execution.

---

1 Wooden, Jevon. "Don't Think of a Sale, Think of a Relationship with Alan Weiss, The Million Dollar Consultant." *Design Your Life and Business: The Leaders Podcast.* Podcast audio, 23 August 2023

Action Steps:

1. Break down each business goal into actionable steps.

2. Delegate tasks to team members based on their skills and strengths.

3. Use data to identify and eliminate inefficiencies in your workflow.

4. Regularly assess whether your resources are aligned with your priorities.

NOTES

NOTES

SECTION III: YARE

The concept of yare is all about making things easier for yourself. The term was originally used in seafaring and describes a vessel that handles easily and responds quickly to the helm. If you turn the wheel a little, the ship responds by turning with ease. In other words, it refers to a smoothly operating ship—the perfect metaphor for running a business effectively.

CHAPTER 6: DELEGATE, DELETE, DELAY

AS BUSINESS OWNERS, ENTREPRENEURS, AND LEADERS, WE OFTEN WANT TO DO *everything* on our ship—and we can't. It can be hard to hand the helm over, even to a trusted first mate. Starting a business means building something out of nothing and advancing into uncharted waters, which, by the way, is the definition of crazy by most people's standards. The leap of faith it takes to start a business begins inside you, in your soul. And often, the questions we ask ourselves are, "How far are you willing to go?" and "How much are you willing to risk?" But in this chapter, we're turning that notion on its head to address the question, "How much are you willing to give up control?" Because entrepreneurship is not simply about being the one on top; it's about accepting that there's a lot you *can't* control. Relinquishing control and internalizing that concept is key if you want to succeed.

In the military, you have to trust the person on your left and your right. You know that person will pick up your slack and watch your back. In battle, this is a matter of life and death; in business, it can mean the life or the death of your company.

We also have another saying in the service: KISS, or keep it simple stupid, which parallels the essence of yare. Do everything in your power to make things easier for you and the people around you—that way, you can focus on the bigger challenges ahead.

Biting off more than you can chew can lead to minor headaches for you and your business, including burnout, stress, and small errors that affect client relationships, and major catastrophes, like being unable to deliver on services or accruing insurmountable debt. The first element of yare—delegate—is designed to prevent this. The "three Ds" of yare are delegate, delete, delay . We will cover these in order in the following sections. The three Ds emphasize that running a business goes beyond what you can do on your own. So, get comfortable with letting things go. Learn to trust others to help get you where you want to go.

If You Delegate Authority, You Will Build Leaders

As a leader, you want to be running your business, not letting the business run you. I know y'all have heard that before. If you followed through, I wouldn't need to say it! So start doing it.

First, identify which tasks can be delegated to your team members or outsourced to freelancers. Outsourcing is a must in business, whether you're a solopreneur or a Fortune 500 company. Make a list of all the tasks that take up your time and energy, and then evaluate which ones can be done by someone else. It's a win-win. You'll have more time to focus on the big picture and key elements of your business, plus that shared responsibility for realizing the mission will help instill a sense of trust and alignment in your employees. People want to feel a sense of ownership—empower them!

While I was in basic training, I severely injured my ankle while practicing jiu-jitsu. When it happened, I felt like a running back getting taken down and crushed under the pile of 230-

pound linemen. Well, if you can't perform on the job, which I no longer could, you get "restarted" in basic training. You have to go back to the very beginning.

During basic, every morning in PT, we did rope climbing, which is more about footwork than upper body strength. Proper footwork allows you to secure a firm hold on the rope, using your legs to push yourself up rather than relying solely on your arms. This technique not only conserves energy but also provides stability. Fearful of being restarted, I didn't want to tell anyone about my busted ankle, but I also couldn't grasp the rope with my ankle. I attempted it anyway, and you guessed it—I dropped like a stone, falling from a pretty serious height and landing on that same ankle.

I learned a lesson the hard way that day: if you need help, tell somebody! Whatever is keeping you from speaking up—fear of the consequences or appearing weak or less than capable—those fears are usually unfounded. The reality is that most people *want* to help. Your employees or freelancers are eager to step up to the plate. I didn't say anything that day because I worried that if I had told my drill sergeant, he would say, "You're a no-good son of a—." But that wasn't his response. Far from it. Instead, he said, "Why the hell didn't you tell me you were injured?"

So don't work against your own interests. Don't defeat yourself. Embrace the fact that people want to assist you. If you've created a positive mission that people want to get behind (as we discussed in Chapter 2), then people will be excited to help you accomplish that vision.

For some of you, delegation might be as natural as breathing, and that's great. You've got a head start on the three Ds. For those of you who are more like me and have trouble letting go, there are different ways of approaching delegation. You can write a list of things you hate to do as a leader. This might include tasks like detailed data entry, responding to routine emails, or managing administrative paperwork. Identifying these items helps determine what you can delegate to free up your time and energy for higher-priority work. That's good fodder for delegation. You might also acknowledge that some things you're just not good at. Maybe you hate administrative work or dread finance and accounting (I know I do). Recognizing these areas helps you identify tasks to delegate and allows you to focus on what you excel at and enjoy doing. Find someone who can do it better and more efficiently than you. When delegating tasks, it is important to consider the strengths and skills of your team members or freelancers. Assign tasks to the person with the proper skill set and sufficient capacity to do the job as well or better than you would yourself. This is especially true for mid-level managers who tend to hold on to too many minute tasks that they should instead be delegating.

The next step is to set clear expectations. Once you have identified the tasks that can be delegated, communicate your expectations clearly. Provide detailed instructions, timelines, and goals to ensure that team members or freelancers understand what is expected of them. This also means you must provide adequate training to ensure the task can be completed effectively. This can be done through workshops, formal training sessions, or online tutorials.

One trick I like to use when it comes to delegation is "talent stashing." The idea originated with sports—you want depth of talent on your bench so that if a first-string player is injured, a competent backup can step in—but the practice now gets applied to various disciplines, from medicine to tech support. Stack your deck with team members and freelancers who you can draw from *before* you get overloaded.

For example, I find sales to be very time-consuming. When I first started my business, I was spending hours every day identifying, qualifying, and calling leads. It was such a drain on my time that I decided to automate the process. However, I quickly realized that automation wasn't enough; there needed to be human judgment to correctly qualify leads and a personal quality to those touches with clients when I did reach out. So, I had to bring on someone to take over those sales-related tasks. Yes, there is a financial cost to every hire, but they are invaluable. They save me time and generate new business.

I'm also reminded of Tanya, the bubbly educational consultant we discussed in Chapter 1. She was so invested in the mission of educating and empowering at-risk youth that she was hesitant to give over any control of her business to anyone else. She was doing everything from making PowerPoint presentations to teaching classes. Her focus was divided, meaning she made mistakes that otherwise would've been caught. She had a lot of enviable strengths and admirable attributes, but she was no good at relinquishing control.

She did have a team that was supposed to handle things like planning courses, creating presentations, and sourcing new opportunities. They simply weren't doing it because *she* was doing all of it. It added to her stress and feeling overwhelmed by her work—of course it did! And that didn't change until she started delegating those tasks. She also brought on an executive assistant to serve as the face of the organization, talk to prime clients, and handle other essential, time-consuming tasks. As a result, she was able to grow her business more efficiently, and she didn't have to take her work home with her every night.

What's in Your Pack?

There is a saying in the army, "Only bring what you can carry." This might seem obvious, but you understand its value when your joints and muscles are groaning amidst the strain of a twelve-mile march with a sixty-pound rucksack in the desert heat! Deletion is all about being real with yourself. What do you *really need* in that rucksack?

In business, we often come up with bright ideas—creating a new product line or partnering with a trending influencer—as a byproduct of our excitement over what we're building and where our business is heading. But sometimes, those ideas spring up before we've done our homework—before we know if that idea will have any real payoff.

Or we cling to an underperforming product line when it would be better to get rid of it. We want to be innovators and creators, but it is essential that key decisions are well-researched and data-driven. And if something is dead weight, get it out of your pack!

For example, at one point I created online courses for business coaching, but marketing them was eating up too much time. I had to be honest with myself—the courses weren't selling, and the resources it took to market them were consuming too much of my budget. The cost/benefit just wasn't there. I had to get rid of them, and I never looked back. No more carrying around dead weight.

The first step in the deletion process is to conduct a deletion audit twice a year. What tasks, ideas, or even employees are underperforming or not contributing meaningfully to your success? It's important to regularly review all the tasks and activities performed within your business to identify any outdated or unnecessary ones. This may include outdated processes, activities no longer aligned with your business goals, or tasks that are time-consuming without providing significant value. By identifying these tasks, you can determine which ones should be eliminated or modified to optimize your business processes.

Utilize thresholds and benchmarks to guide your decision-making process. If a product or service hasn't met its benchmark in two years, you should probably give it the axe. In Chapter 4, we discussed the importance of having the right people on your team doing the right job. Your people strategy should also be subject to these reviews—but this *doesn't* necessarily mean giving them the axe in the same way as a task. These are your people! You've invested in them, and they've invested in you.

If people aren't fulfilling their KPIs, perhaps try job rotation. See how they perform in a different role or under a different management strategy. I often suggest that clients offer employees "a day in the life" type exercises to learn about other aspects of the business and see what opportunities they might like to explore. This can include cross-training, cross-collaborating, and allowing people to try new roles, all of which also open possibilities for advancement. If all else fails and someone really isn't pulling their weight, then and only then consider termination.

Once you've identified the tasks that are no longer necessary, it's important to prioritize your remaining tasks based on their importance. This will help you determine which tasks are essential to achieving your business goals and which ones can be eliminated without negatively impacting operations. High-priority tasks might include strategic planning, client relationship management, revenue-generating activities, and team leadership. By focusing on these high-priority tasks, you improve efficiency and productivity and achieve better results with fewer resources— exactly what you should strive to do as a business owner.

You might also consider whether there are alternative ways to achieve the same goal without completing the task. In some cases, it may be possible to achieve the same outcome without completing a specific task. For example, if a task involves manual data entry, it may be possible to automate the process using technology. Or, to return to the story about my broken ankle, another obstacle for me during basic training was the PT test, which involved a two-mile run. There I was with a jacked ankle on crutches, looking pathetic as hell. The drill sergeant took one look at me and said, "And how do you think you're going to do this?"

You cannot get help on the PT test or advance from basic training if you don't pass it. I had no choice. I had to figure out how to do it despite the excruciating pain. So I found my "rabbit," someone who was a little slower than me and could pace me. I knew that if I stayed with him to the end, I would make it. I would sprint, then walk a little to let my ankle rest. Sprint, then walk, staying right on the other guy's tail until the final minute sprint. And I passed the PT test. The lesson there was this: be smart about how you approach challenges. If something isn't going your way, there is always another option. Sometimes, you just have to be creative, and sometimes, you just have to find your rabbit.

"Delayed Is Preferable to Never"[2]

Not every underperforming task or aspect of your business must be delegated or deleted. Sometimes, the proper course is to delay. That bright idea that hit you in the shower might not work for your business today, but it could be better implemented in a year or more down the line. Prioritize what you want to achieve in business and what timeline to follow. Anything that isn't necessary for achieving immediate goals can perhaps be pushed back. Think of it like having a few tricks up your sleeve or a dish on the backburner you can fire when ready.

---

2 Danish proverb.

For example, say you run a software company and need another coder to help with a new program with a release date two years from now. That second coder is not an urgent need; you might delay that hire until you have the revenue to better afford them. You have better cash flow in the meantime for investment and expenses, and when you do make the move for a new hire, you might be able to offer a more competitive salary and attract even better talent.

When it comes to "delaying," identify tasks that are important but not urgent. These tasks may not have immediate deadlines, but they are essential to the success of the business in the long run. This might include developing a new product line, improving customer service processes, or building relationships with new clients. To help determine which tasks should be prioritized, classify them based on their urgency and importance: 1) urgent and important; 2) important but not urgent; 3) not important and not urgent. Prioritize tasks that are urgent and important first, followed by tasks that are important but not urgent.

For example, imagine you own a digital marketing agency. You've landed a major campaign for a big client. You also want to rebrand the company, but your resources are consumed with client work. Which one should you prioritize? A rebrand will interrupt your current workflow. So, wait until the campaign is over, then tackle the rebrand. By delaying non-urgent tasks, you can free up time to focus on urgent tasks that require immediate attention.

However, it's essential to ensure that delayed tasks do not pile up and create a backlog. This ties back in with one of the other three Ds: delegate. If you have tasks you've identified as important but not urgent, delegate them! That way, they will get done without taking up your precious time and bandwidth.

The bottom line is to be honest with yourself—about your capacity, likes and dislikes, what you can realistically accomplish on your own, and, critically, what you need help with. By delegating, deleting, and delaying tasks, you'll find your ship cutting seamlessly through the waters ahead. To make things even easier, the next solution we'll talk about is automation.

NOTES

CHAPTER 7: AUTOMATION

THERE ARE PLENTY OF THINGS ABOUT RUNNING A BUSINESS THAT ARE HARD—*really hard.* Thankfully, we live in an era of technology, and many of the most tiring aspects of entrepreneurship now have technological solutions. Automation means simplicity, and as a business owner, simplicity is your best friend. This is the second aspect of yare: getting your ship running smoothly and sleekly through the sometimes treacherous waters of small business ownership.

Of course, automation should not and cannot displace the necessary human components of a business. We've all been on the receiving end of an automated customer service hotline or chatbot that takes you in circles through useless FAQ pages or extension options. And hopefully, we've all had the experience of someone answering the call, resolving the issue quickly and kindly, and saving us a lot of time, stress, and trouble. Humans are sometimes the more efficient and valuable option. And don't think you need to automate things for the sake of automation or to appear on the cutting edge. Automate processes because there is a specific problem to solve or improve. Automation is a tool, a means to an end rather than an end in itself.

So, how do you determine what processes to automate? What steps do you need to take before implementation? And—

you should be able to guess the next step—how do you track the success of automation?

To Automate or Not to Automate, That Is the Question

Automation is the next logical step following a three Ds audit. By now, you've identified tasks that are time-consuming or repetitive. An alternative to delegating, deleting, or delaying is automating. As a quick side note, since automation and delegation can sometimes seem similar, the difference between automation, especially when using a person, and delegation is that with delegation, there are still checks and balances; there is some modicum of supervision. That is not the case with automation, even people-driven automation. With automation, the people you outsource to are basically self-regulating. You're not managing them. You just trust that they're doing the work. There are exceptions, but the point is to set the ball in motion and let physics do the rest.

So, when it comes to automation, take a close look at your daily workflow and identify tasks that take up too much time or are done on a regular basis. These might include data entry, scheduling appointments, or sending follow-up emails. Then, evaluate whether there are tools or software that can automate those tasks.

I spoke with Shaun Whynacht on this subject. Shaun is the CEO of Blue Cow Marketing, and he's passionate about small business ownership. The entrepreneurial spirit is practically woven into his DNA. Upon completing his college studies in television production, he spent more than a decade exploring every corner of Canada and learning about the business world as an employee. He's seen it all, from non-profits to corporations and revenue development to web design.

Something he said in our conversation that really struck me was this: "Our attention spans, our patience as a consumer is getting shorter and shorter. When somebody requests something on your website or sends you a message, we often have this feeling or this need that we should be instantly replying back to them. So, if you can't, you need to set that expectation for when you can. So you automate the follow-up and automate the expectations, and this can really give the best customer experience possible."[3] It comes down to expectations and customer experience. If you're not sure about whether to automate, put yourself in your customers' shoes and think about what you would expect in a given situation. Then, address those needs and expectations.

A good way to determine tasks for automation is the rock, pebble, sand test for time management. Rocks are tasks that are important, albeit time-consuming, but they are non-negotiable and must be done. Pebbles need to be done, but not necessarily by you or immediately. They are good candidates for delegation to marketers or content creators. Remember that automation is not always technological; sometimes, you can have people automating processes. Lastly, sand tasks are usually simple processes

---

3 Wooden, Jevon. "The True, Life-Changing Power of Automation with Shaun Whynacht, CEO of Blue Cow Marketing." *Design Your Life and Business: The Leaders Podcast.* Podcast audio, 24 October 2023. https://theleaderspod.com/e/68rmk05n-the-true-life-changing-power-of-automation-with-shaun-whynacht

that are done regularly and predictably and can be fairly tedious or repetitive. These are "set it and forget it" tasks, and they are ideal for automation, like an autogenerated welcome email to people who sign up for your website newsletter.

Prime candidates for automation for most businesses include CRM functions, repetitive email sequences (like lead generation and welcome sequences that are part of your funnel), outreach through platforms like LinkedIn, and segmenting. Keep in mind that automation does not mean the process has to be impersonal. For example, if you want to automate outreach messages from LinkedIn, you can still personalize them. Automate it with a tool that parses information from company profiles and adds it to your message: "Hi [NAME], I noticed that [COMPANY] is serving in the marketing industry. I'd love to talk to you about your goals." Little touches that make it feel less like a canned or spam communication can make all the difference. The same is true for segmenting. Pinpoint the reason why that specific person is receiving that specific message. Don't just spray and pray. Find ways to keep the human component alive. You want to sound like *you*—not like ChatGPT. And you want your customers to feel heard and valued.

Despite being a massive advocate for automation, Shaun acknowledged that there is such a thing as too much of it. "I strongly feel that automation is never going to replace us; it is something that is going to work beside us," he said.4 If you lose who you are as a brand or person, you likely have tipped the

---

4 Ibid.

balance of scales too far in favor of automation. Signs that this is the case are when those personal touches start to go the wayside or when you start creating content that doesn't fit your brand's mission and values. It's all about moderation because automation is, ultimately, just a tool, and someone needs to wield it.

Map It Out

Once you've identified tasks that can be automated, do some research to find software or tools that can help you. For example, there are tools available that can automatically schedule social media posts or software that can automate your accounting processes.

Before you automate, ask yourself, *Who is this serving? Who is the end user, and how will they benefit?* Imagine you are planning to implement scheduling software. Clients have given you feedback that indicates they would benefit from a reminder system—something to automatically notify you and them of upcoming appointments, events, or courses. But you also don't want clients to feel overwhelmed by too many notifications. Ask whether what you're automating will improve things for you and the client—and *how*.

I like to use white boards and mind maps to think through automation. Walk through the process that you plan to automate step by step. Make sure it's logical and coherent. For example, if someone signs up for an online course, and you've automated the site to play all the videos automatically, the viewer is going to be overwhelmed and probably walk away. Instead, it would make more sense to drip feed access to subscribers so they can build skills and knowledge as they work their way through your course. Or you might design it so they can bounce between modules depending on their experience and ability. They might only be interested in specific parts of the course rather than the course as a whole.

One method for evaluating how a process should ideally run is to assess whether a "waterfall" or "agile" approach would be more beneficial to end users. This method comes from project management theory. With a waterfall approach, the user or program must finish one step or phase before moving on to the next. You must complete A before moving on to B. In an agile approach, which emphasizes flexibility and adaptability, the user or program moves as necessary. Processes can be cyclical rather than linear, allowing teams to iterate and make adjustments as they go. You can jump from A to D to B to Q, doing what needs to be done in that moment to respond to changing needs or priorities. This iterative and responsive nature defines an agile approach and makes it well-suited for environments where quick adaptation is key.

The final step before implementation is testing. Like I've said before, measure twice, cut once. Before automating any process, be sure to test it before launch. Simulate an alternate environment to test whatever you're about to put out. For example, if you're on WordPress, you can use a "staging site," which is not live but allows you to test on the back end and see how things work on the front end before you publish and go live. For emails, try A/B testing your automation process.

Once you've found a tool or software that can automate a task, implement it into your workflow. Make sure to train your team on how to use the tool and monitor its effectiveness over time. By automating tasks, you can save time and reduce errors, ultimately increasing productivity and profitability.

The Accountants

When I first started BrightMind Consulting Group, I worked with a two-person accounting firm. They were doing well, but they were also doing everything manually. If someone went to their website, they'd have to call, and the owners would handle all the correspondence. They also did their own bookkeeping and filed their own taxes. Everything was word of mouth. There was no lead generation from their end.

This was a clear opportunity to divest of some time-consuming tasks. First, we set up an automatic email reply letting interested potential clients and existing ones know, "We'll get back to you within twenty-four hours." This meant that they were able to schedule blocks of time to reply to inquiries rather than having their daily workflow interrupted by calls. We also added a form to the website and a couple of lead magnets to give clients a chance to get to know the company without talking directly to the owners, reducing the amount of time the owners had to spend on prospects that might not pan out.

To bolster the personal element of their newly created funnel, we implemented a welcome sequence for website visitors. We still included the phone number for folks who wanted to call right away, but there was material supplementing it that often answered most of their questions and allayed common concerns. They hired a small firm that provided round-the-clock customer service. It was a small cost to them and greatly bolstered their customer service ratings. They had the option to scale it up and down as *they* needed, but it was especially important during their busy season in increasing the number of "closes" they made of new clients.

They were also producing their own content manually. They mainly used LinkedIn since they were a B2B accounting firm, focusing on content such as industry insights, financial tips, thought leadership articles, and case studies. We implemented a tool that let them schedule content publication weeks and months out, so they didn't have to scramble week to week to write something for publication. They "batched" their content—creating a coherent series over a couple of days—then scheduled it out ahead of time.

It led to a better book of business, greater customer satisfaction (because they had more time), and lower customer turnover, and they avoided having to hire unnecessary staff because they could automate some functions. They were able to focus on more valuable work and provide clients with better service because their time was no longer eaten up by the minutia of administration. Automation elevated their whole stature as a business.

Track the Tech

By now, you know I love a tracking system. Tracking gives you the proof in the pudding, the rich data you need to be certain you're spending your precious resources wisely. If a process is automated and you're no longer involved in it day to day, how do you know it's working? The success of automation doesn't just lie in speed or efficiency; it's also about the value delivered to your customers. Of course, as we've discussed, every business has its own yardstick. What you track will depend on what you've automated and what matters most to your business. Ask yourself, *Why am I automating? What checks and balances do I need to put in place to make sure the automation is doing what I need it to do?*

If you want to reduce lead time or increase conversion rates using automated processes, be sure to track that! If you want to reduce the amount of unplanned work (like the accountants), track it! Your tracking system can be a simple spreadsheet or a very advanced tool designed to track and measure key metrics (like Meta Business).

Another important reason to track automations is that automations do stop—sometimes for no apparent rhyme or reason. Maybe a piece of code changed, or the software updated and left your website behind. I've seen businesses automate a summit or workshop, but the link was bad, and no one could access it. And if you're trying to woo clients, it doesn't leave a good impression if they think you're cutting corners with sloppy technology. So, set alerts that will notify you of system failures.

Ultimately, automation should facilitate building rapport and relationships. It saves time and reduces errors. "To err is human," but to automate is divine. People get tired. We make mistakes. Maybe it's a typo in your email blast or a period in the wrong place in your accounting books. These things happen, but they happen a lot less when you automate.

So far, we've covered the yardstick, yield, and yare of the 5Y Framework. In the next section, we'll move on to yoga and how to make your business flexible and adaptable so you can take advantage of every opportunity for growth.

Section Summary:

- Simplified processes reduce stress and increase agility in your business.

- Flexibility and ease of use make it easier to adapt to challenges.

- Streamlined systems save time and money while enhancing efficiency.

Action Steps:

1. Identify one complex process in your business and map out its steps.

2. Look for redundancies or bottlenecks and brainstorm ways to simplify the process.

3. Explore tools or technology that can automate repetitive tasks.

4. Implement one simplification strategy and measure its impact on productivity.

NOTES

SECTION IV: YOGA

In this section, you can expect to gain an in-depth understanding of how to cultivate flexibility, sustainability, and scalability within your business. The material will guide you on the importance of adapting to change, staying innovative, and approaching challenges with an experimental mindset. It highlights how being agile and open to pivots can strengthen your business's capacity to thrive in evolving environments.

You'll also explore how embedding sustainable practices at every level can ensure long-term success, supported by a culture of empathy and responsible decision-making. Finally, the section delves into strategies for scaling your business effectively, emphasizing the need for strong foundations, a reliable team, and the right timing. By integrating these principles, you'll be equipped to build a resilient business that not only grows but does so with purpose and sustainability.

CHAPTER 8: FLEXIBILITY

WHEN YOU IMAGINE A YOGI, YOU PROBABLY PICTURE SOMEONE WHO CAN CONTORT THEM-
selves into positions most of us strain to even think of, and they make it look graceful. They've got their legs over their head and arms wrapped behind their back, yet they remain calm, no matter how strenuous the position. A yogi is dedicated to practicing until they can move with ease. They can hold positions but also flow. Most crucially, they find the balance between flexibility and strength.

Personally, yoga has helped me through various injuries and the PTSD I experienced after returning home from Afghanistan. Yoga helped me rebuild my strength, but it also enabled me to improve my mobility, range of motion, and, of course, flexibility. It's hard as hell—some days it takes everything to show up to the mat— and I'm not the best at it, but I stick with it. Sometimes, the best thing to do is bend to the discipline. And that is another interesting dynamic of yoga: the counterintuitive notion that dis-cipline can lead to fluidity and flexibility.

There are three key elements to flexibility: being open to pivoting, embracing experimentation, and fostering a culture of innovation. If you can do that, you'll be well on your way to becoming a business yogi.

The Pivotal Pivot

In yoga, sometimes the smallest adjustment is what you need to unlock a pose: relaxing your shoulder blades, releasing your breath, or twisting from your hips. Other times, we might need to totally change the way we get into a pose or get help to reach the full expression of a posture. Business is no different. To survive and thrive, businesses need to make adjustments, big and small, and sometimes we need outside help. (Here you are, reading this book!)

Even the best-laid plans can go awry, and businesses that are rigidly set in their ways may struggle to adapt. By staying flexible and being willing to pivot when necessary, businesses can adjust to changing market conditions, customer needs, and other factors that may impact growth. This might involve shifting your focus to a new product or service, targeting a different demographic, or exploring new marketing channels.

A pivot is a decision; in business, we often make decisions emotionally instead of rationally or objectively. But business decisions should be grounded in the data. And don't decide in a vacuum. Listen to what the market is telling you, what customers are telling you, what employees are telling you.

When I pivoted my business, I looked at the data. The former name, Live Not Loathe, is a nice mantra to live by, but as a brand, it's vague and does not convey our service offerings. I conducted a survey and asked people, "What does the name mean to you?" The old name made people think more of personal development coaching, not business coaching—and I wanted to focus on business coaching. I also queried people with different alternative names, and the results told me the pivot would pay off.

BrightMind Consulting Group reminded people not only of business consulting but also of leadership, ideas, and flipping the switch. The verdict was in. A change of name would clarify my services and improve sound lead generation. I didn't pivot it because I was excited about a name or gravitated to one because it sounded nice. The decision was backed by data and customer feedback.

"Let go" is one of the most common phrases in yoga. Teachers use it to cue letting go of any tension in the body or your breath or negative thoughts. When we pivot in business, we must learn to let go of ideas we thought were great or revolutionary. It's not always easy, but it is necessary to grow.

Keep It Loose and Channel Your Inner Scientist

Flexibility in business growth often means taking calculated risks. One way to do this is by experimenting with new strategies, products, or services on a smaller scale before committing significant resources. This allows you to test the waters and gather valuable feedback before making a larger investment. For example, you might launch a pilot program in a particular region or market segment before expanding it nationally. Give yourself options.

In my own business, I launched a course when I first started. I had been listening to the so-called gurus who told coaches a course was essential to launching your public profile. But sales were flat. And I mean flat—I think I sold the course to a whopping *two* businesses—despite having marketed it aggressively. I know now that what I had failed to do was 1) gather information beforehand on what the market wanted and 2) allow myself flexibility. I had created it "my way"—within rigid margins—and it fell flat. What I learned is what I apply now to clients. Before I do anything, I get insight and gather data. Then, start small so that if a product or service doesn't pan out, your business avoids taking a big hit. Don't bite off more than you can chew.

You might remember the personal trainer, Sean, from Chapter 1, whom I coached. Sean was struggling to build his client base. He imagined training other college or professional athletes like himself, but there wasn't any demand from that segment of the market. We tested a number of variables: client demographics, class size, and class type. The results showed that younger, highly athletic clients were less interested in structured group classes, while middle-aged clients valued the social and motivational aspects of group training. Additionally, smaller class sizes fostered more engagement and higher satisfaction, but larger classes were more profitable when balanced with slightly reduced per-person charges. Based on these findings, I determined that group training would be most effective. By first setting out Sean's revenue goals and then reverse engineering the class size and per-person charge that would meet those goals, we were able to create a viable plan. Sean would need to focus on a different clientele—not pro athletes but normal, middle-aged women who valued community and supportive fitness environments. He would need to pivot from linebackers to Lululemon. There's no surprise ending here—as you found out in Chapter 1, the pivot paid off because we based decisions on sound research.

In yoga, you have to listen to your body. In business, you have to listen to the market. Flexibility isn't just about you. You have to do the simple poses before you do the hard ones. And sometimes, that means putting your ego aside. But you also won't know how far you can stretch into a pose if you don't try. So, embrace experimentation. Take a deep breath, go slowly, and twist a little deeper. Like all things in yoga, you are striving for balance—between what you can do now and what you are working toward.

Innovation Station

If businesses want to remain flexible and adaptable, they must foster a culture of innovation. This means encouraging employees to share their ideas and insights, experimenting with new approaches, and rewarding creativity and problem-solving. When employees feel empowered to take risks and try new things, they're more likely to identify opportunities for growth and take advantage of them.

It's easy to be consumed with the demand of daily duties, which means people doing the everyday work—who know the job in and out, who are best positioned to identify areas of weakness or opportunities for growth—aren't thinking strategically. That is why giving your people—and yourself—space and time for thought, innovation, and creativity is so important.

Google encourages employees to follow the 20 percent rule: they should spend 20 percent of their working hours generating ideas on how to improve the company. The concept is so central to their company culture that it was enshrined in their founder's IPO letter when the company went public. Now, you might not be operating on the same scale as Google, but you can encourage employees to formulate one or two goals per year that they must figure out how to attain. That gives them the chance to challenge themselves *and* the status quo.

Or take Amazon as an example. Amazon doesn't do traditional brainstorming sessions. Instead, they employ "retrograde analysis," a form of strategic thinking that works backward from the customer or end goal (like I did with Sean). They've found that it leads to reduced spending in the initial stages of a project or product and clarifies the process for key players. There's no wasting time writing a thousand raw ideas on a board. Most importantly, it centers their clients, meaning they know from the start a new product or line will be successful.

I use feedback from one-on-one client sessions to tweak the leadership coaching program and make it better. For example, in addition to just one-hour sessions, I can do fifteen-minute "laser focus sessions": no bull, very efficient sessions. We focus on what the client wants to talk about. They're to the point, with no dead space. Some common points clients often want to discuss include a lack of confidence, a lack of clarity around their goals or next steps, and strategies for communicating effectively with their teams. These laser sessions allow us to quickly zero in on these recurring challenges and uncover hidden client needs that might not surface in longer, more general discussions. That focus has made a big difference in my coaching practice and has helped me address specific pain points that resonate with many of my clients.

Focus groups are another great way to drive innovation. Create a safe environment where people can voice opinions, including unconventional or even controversial ones. Then, give people the responsibility to execute the ideas generated in the focus group. Some people need that time to think it over and process it out of the office; they think best while walking or making dinner. And this allows different personality types to contribute and breaks down silos.

I was hired to speak at a university in Georgia on the subject of allowing diverse thinking. Usually, with diversity, we think about racial, ethnic, or gender diversity. Diverse thinking also refers to diverse experiences and varied outlooks on life and business. A common problem I hear from executives is that they are subjected to endless meetings that don't generate any meaningful change or result. When you have the same person running the meeting or setting the agenda, people fall into patterns of behavior—maybe they feel stymied or like they need to agree with whatever idea is being floated. It's even worse today with remote work and Zoom meetings, where people don't feel as connected to the work or workplace.

However, we can free ourselves from groupthink patterns by allowing individuals to share their experiences, putting them in the driver's seat, and giving them the opportunity to lead or offer solutions. I encourage using "rotating chairs" so that people other than the department leader or CEO have the chance to head meetings. The facilitator changes week to week. This shakes things up and helps identify potential leaders who might be prime candidates for managerial roles. The Socratic method is another useful tool. Scrutinize everything. Use doubt as a tool of exploration. If the CEO says, "Hey, let's launch a new product," you don't want yes-men to blindly approve the move; you want hard thinkers to ask the tough questions like, *Why? Who does this serve? Do we really need this?*

Innovation doesn't have to be grand, seismic, or even radically new. You can borrow ideas, make a small tweak, and thus create something new. Look at the Apple iPhone series. Each new model is by and large the same as the last, with a few new features and modifications, but it always sells.

Where Does Flexibility Lead?

When I was deployed, my body started to break down, and I realized that tech wasn't my true passion. The physical strain I was experiencing made me more introspective, forcing me to question what I was truly passionate about and what I wanted from life. Despite having developed an extensive skillset in IT and knowing the vast opportunities for professionals in the field, I found that it didn't ignite any sense of fulfillment or joy. The breakdown of my body served as a metaphor for how I felt internally—pushing through something that was no longer sustainable or aligned with my true desires. People had told me I was a great motivator and mentor. I was a natural at encouraging people to achieve their best selves. So, I thought, *How could I earn money from this?* While still on active duty, I did some research and came upon coaching. I completed my certification through the International Coaching Federation. At first, I conceptualized it through a sports lens, the way a coach imposes a method to train the players. I approached change as top-down. However, I quickly realized that that method did not work for me or my clients. Again, I pivoted. The coaching I do is not prescriptive. I do my best to guide clients toward answers without dictating or controlling their choices.

Initially, I was coaching soldiers for free, as a kind of training for myself and as a means of support for them. Being away from home in a foreign and hostile environment can be stressful. It's very limiting. You can't just cruise around town and hang out. People struggle to stay positive, overcome homesickness, and deal with the stress of deployment. These concerns are not unique to service members, however. They go to the heart of being human, slippery existential problems that are difficult to grapple with—problems that won't sit still in your mind long enough to get a clear picture, that transform into a nagging sense of dread. There is not always a clear answer. Even as a coach, it can be difficult to know, but if you know what questions to ask, you can lead people to insight or enlightenment.

And then the bombing at the base happened—the major turning point in my life. The base was on heightened alert after the incident because there are often waves of attacks in events like this. Luckily, that was the only attack that day. In the aftermath, I was part of the remains cleanup team. I was picking up body parts and putting them in trash bags. It may sound harsh, but it's important to clear the scene quickly. As I power-washed blood and remains from the concrete, I checked in on my fellow comrades, making sure they were holding up amidst the shock and trauma. The impact of that day was profound—it shattered any illusion I had about invincibility and forced me to confront the raw reality of life and death. It changed how I viewed my purpose, making me deeply reconsider what I was doing with my life and pushing me to find meaning beyond the chaos and violence of war. This experience planted the seed for pursuing a path that would allow me to help others heal and grow and ultimately led me toward coaching and training.

People were shaken up. I thought I was ok. It was only a matter of days before the base went back to normal operations. I resumed my day-to-day work. I was traveling around Afghanistan. Other bases I visited were attacked during the subsequent days. There were attempts to breach base walls, constant mortar shelling, and more suicide attacks. I was on edge, but I told myself, "Hey, I'm trained for this."

Six months later, I was home and having terrible nightmares. I was there, living the events of November 12. Every night, the same nightmare: the flash of red, the cleanup team, and an explosion; then I woke up.

After a month of nightmares and terrible sleep, I thought, *I can't do this. This sucks.* I felt detached. I couldn't enjoy anything. At that point, I was in the Reserves and had returned to my civilian job as if nothing had happened. I didn't speak about the bombing, my nightmares, or how I was feeling with anyone. How could I? Who could understand what I saw, what I went through? I felt really down. I started having suicidal ideation.

One day, I called my older sister. "I'm sorry if I wasn't there for my nephew or for you," I said. I rambled on, trying to get it all off my chest.

My sister said two words: "Get help."

Growing up in my culture and growing up poor, I was taught to suck it up and move forward. But my sister showed me I didn't have to wear that Superman cape. I could be Clark Kent. Those two words put me on a new path.

I started therapy. In Afghanistan, I was studying for my certification in coaching, so I knew about the field. I remember the therapist asked me something that changed my whole mindset as I told her about the nightmares, the cold sweats, and the lurking feeling of dread.

"Did you die?" she asked. "Did you die in that dream? What happens next?"

"I have no idea," I said.

She said, "You feel guilty because you're still here. And you have some unfinished business in real life."

I realized that I hadn't reached out to anyone I had deployed with. Of the bonds and friendships I had made over three deployments, I had lost over 20 people to suicide after their return home. These were people who had lost their sense of belonging and their place in the world, people who felt they were undeserving of love or lacked the love and purpose they so desperately needed. They were unmoored.

It's a grave problem. According to the organization Stop Soldier Suicide, founded by three Army veterans who, like me, had lost friends they had served with to suicide, six thousand vets kill themselves each year. Servicemembers have a 57 percent higher risk of suicide than the general population, and the risk is even higher for those who have deployed.[5]

I started posting wellness checks to anyone I was in touch with on social media. Camaraderie is important. It's our sense of purpose and our sense of love that drives people. That is true on both a personal and professional level. You never know what people are going through. Some of the seemingly happiest folks, people who always have a smile on their faces, are the ones struggling the most. And the worst injuries are often the scars we can't see.

A lot of people say, "I don't need a coach. I'm good. I'm doing what I want." To that, I would say all the greats had a coach to get them to where they need to be—Ali, Jordan, Serena Williams. Even at the top of their game, they had a coach. A coach often helps you see what's possible. The real peak of the mountain might be shrouded in mist. Coaching helps you along your climb and gives you the strength to push through to the summit. I saw the energy and invigoration, the confidence and productivity boost that came from coaching. Those results encouraged me to continue down this path.

I received the Bronze Star for my actions in the aftermath of the bombing on November 12, 2016, but that's one medal I wish I could give back. We lost many people, and many more were physically and emotionally injured. But that day changed my life and set me on the path to becoming a coach.

---

5 "Veteran Suicide Stats," Stop Soldier Suicide, n.d., https:// stopsoldiersuicide.org/vet-stats

A detonation is a flash, a split-second in time—and it causes a lifetime of pain. Your actions, no matter how brief, have a lifetime impact, especially if you're in a leadership position. So, will your impact be positive, or will it be a detriment?

NOTES

CHAPTER 9: SUSTAINABILITY

YOGA IS A DISCIPLINE THAT REQUIRES PRACTICE, AND THAT PRACTICE MUST BE SUSTAIN-able. By "sustainable," I mean it should be balanced and maintainable over the long term without causing harm or burnout. You might want to get your leg behind your head, but if you force it, rush it, or neglect all the other aspects of your life to get there, you're headed for failure—or, at the very least, a pulled hamstring. Business is the same. It's great to have short-term goals that keep you motivated, but sustainability is about long-term success. No matter what you're building or growing, you want to be able to keep that going well into the future.

When I started my coaching business, I was hyper-focused on the heart work. I wanted to help people, but many people who needed my help the most couldn't afford to pay me. It was costing *me* money to coach people! It took me time to learn that your ideal client must also be able to afford your services. You have to value yourself and your service if you want to stay in business.

I pivoted (remember our friend the pivot?) from people who were in dire need to targeting business leaders who understood the kind of service I offered, the value that came with my services, and who had the budget for it. If I hadn't made that change, I would have gone under. Hell, I would probably have had to go back to IT and to a job I found unfulfilling. But that shift enabled me to build a platform where I can now do both—help the leaders and those most in need—because I pursued sustainable growth.

Whether it's the ethos or economics of your business, sustainable practices are anything that helps future-proof your business and adds value for customers. People want to align with other people and businesses that share similar values. We ended the last chapter by talking about what kind of impact you want to have. In this chapter, we'll look at some ways you can implement practices across your business to ensure your impact is not just a positive one but a sustainable one, too.

Empathy Isn't Just a Word, It's an Action

As a service-based business, there are a few easy steps you can take to improve your environmental sustainability. This includes using eco-friendly products, reducing waste, adopting renewable energy sources, and implementing environmentally friendly business policies. By doing so, businesses can reduce their environmental impact while also appealing to a growing customer base that prioritizes sustainability. The changes might be small at first. Go digital—if you aren't already—by implementing paperless record-keeping or using cloud accounting software. Consider a cycle-to-work scheme or offer a flexible work schedule to reduce the impact of transport. Swap out single-use paper towels or coffee pods in the office for reusable alternatives.

However, what I think is key and what I encourage clients to focus on when it comes to sustainability is *giving*. Giving back to the community shows customers and the wider community that you're serious about your mission and values. It's a win-win. You're doing something good while simultaneously raising your profile. The social impact of your business has a direct correlation with your ability to attract and maintain clients. People increasingly go out of their way to patronize businesses that align with who they are and what they value. What you stand for is an essential part of your brand.

Of course, there is no one-size-fits-all for businesses, but if social responsibility is part of your brand, it can generate business and increase your profitability. Take Patagonia, the outdoor outfitters. Environmental action and sustainability are core to their mission and values, and it's one of the reasons they can charge fifty dollars for a t-shirt.

As you might have gathered from the bits and pieces of my own story, I have a lot of people and opportunities to be grateful for, and at the heart of everything I do is the desire to pay that forward. To that extent, since ensuring my own business is sustainable and generating regular revenue, I have set a mission for BrightMind Consulting Group to help one million minority-owned, woman-owned, and veteran-owned businesses achieve $100,000 in profit.

I mentor a few such businesses pro bono a couple of months a year through a fantastic program called MicroMentor. I speak to thousands of budding entrepreneurs through Verizon's Small Business Digital Ready Program and Community Connect. I also do speaking engagements, in particular for veterans and youth. One of the best parts of those engagements is hearing the student pitches at the end of the seminar. There are truly some bright minds out there! And last, I do a lot of work in prisons. Time is often the best resource we can give because it shows you care—*someone* cares. Through the Prison Entrepreneurship Program in Houston, I teach inmates with less than three years remaining on their sentences about business skills, research strategies and tools, and how to create business plans and pitches. It gives them something to work toward and plan for when they get out. It gives them something to hope for.

Empathy is more than a word. Empathy is about how you engage with people and the world around you. So, put your social impact at the forefront of what you do. Be transparent. Take a position on social causes and communicate that publicly and clearly. But don't just engage in empty sloganeering. Consumers are smart and wary. People will sniff you out if they think you're just trying to capitalize on causes you aren't truly invested in.

Be transparent and think of that transparency as another one of your services. Be transparent with your offerings, price structures, your successes, and, yes, your failures. If you make a mistake, own it. Don't try to spin it. Use it as a way to learn, grow, and move forward. It's not enough to talk the talk; you've got to walk the walk. Customers will know whether you're being authentic. The goal is to live your principles. (A little side-note: the silver lining is that *you* will feel good about your work knowing that you serve a bigger purpose than profits alone.)

Build Sustainability at Every Level

One of the driving messages of this book is the power of people. That includes you, your employees, and your clients and prospects. The other critical element of sustainability in a business model is fostering a culture of sustainability within your organization. Educate employees on sustainable practices (even if right now it's only you!), encourage them to adopt sustainable behaviors, and incorporate sustainability into the business's core values and mission. By doing so, you create a culture of sustainability that drives innovation, enhances customer satisfaction, and promotes long-term success.

Larger companies often have a sustainability officer, and smaller companies can emulate that. You may not have the resources to make it a full-time role, but you no doubt have someone on staff who would be keen to take it on as a side project. Or make it part of the annual training day. Ask yourself and your team, "What does sustainability mean to you?" Open the floor for discussion and see what great ideas your team comes up with. Talk about both kinds of sustainability—environmental sustainability and business longevity. You'll discover new ways to improve your business and empower your employees, which we know leads to greater alignment, job satisfaction, and higher productivity.

As your employees bring that mindset into the workplace and in interactions with clients, your customer service will benefit, as will your longevity. We talked about implementing technological solutions in the section on "yare," but make sure you don't remove all the human elements of your business. If you've ever been in "Facebook jail" or had a flight canceled at the last minute, you'll know how much better it would be if there were just a number you could call and speak to a human—instead of clicking through a thousand online options, none of which can provide you the solution you need. You don't want to be that type of business, no matter how big you get. You want people to feel that emotional connection to your brand.

Gamifying is another great way to build a sustainable business because it makes it fun to do business with you; people will want to engage with you. Offer badges or create loyalty programs. It's not about the monetary value for customers; it's the idea of exclusivity. People want to feel acknowledged and special.

Airlines are a great example of this. Consumers tend to be very brand loyal to airlines they earn miles or points with. Perks like exclusive pre-flight lounge areas and priority boarding don't cost the airlines much in the long run, and they go a long way to boosting customer retention. Provide exclusive content or one-to-one time with the founder as an incentive to members. And remember that membership fees are a predictable, consistent revenue stream—whether it's monthly, semi-annual, or annual—which means you can confidently build toward your long-term goals.

Similarly, offering bundled services can be effective, especially if the add-ons are part of your value ladder. For example, I might offer a client a standalone assessment of their business for X amount. Still, if they enroll in a full coaching package, I offer the initial assessment for free as part of the bundled service package. Just make sure it makes sense for your business model.

Dynamic pricing is another way to make your business more sustainable. What does that mean exactly? Every business is going to have busy and slow quarters, peaks and valleys. If you run a lawn care service, consider lowering prices during off-peak seasons and then adjust accordingly when demand spikes in the spring and summer. Or broaden your services. Can you offer snow-blowing services in winter to your summer landscaping clients? If you provide accounting software, you might change your pricing based on tax return season. Can you offer introductory investment services around Christmas for people who want to get their kids or grandkids investing early? Adapting to seasonality helps ensure you have a consistent flow of customers. (This is yoga, after all—get in the flow!) Again, to do this effectively, you must know your customers' demands and what the market is. It all goes back to data and research.

And lastly, apply the principle of think local, act global. This isn't just about your carbon footprint. If you're like me, you have customers or connections all over the world. You don't have to be a big multinational corporation to do that. We live in a global society, and many businesses reflect that. Whether it's a supply chain from China, a call center in the Philippines, or a data hub in Dubai, it's important to be sensitive to local cultures and norms.

I mentored a female entrepreneur who led a woman-owned start-up in Africa. She was operating in a highly patriarchal environment, and I had to keep that in mind as we explored what opportunities would work best for her and what advantages she might leverage to grow her business. Through our exploration, she identified partnerships with local women's organizations and positioned her business as a champion of community empowerment, which resonated strongly with her target audience. She also learned to navigate and build strategic alliances with influential figures who supported gender equality, allowing her to gain credibility and support within the business community. Ultimately, she was able to operate successfully by aligning her business with values of empowerment and social impact, carving out a niche that allowed her to thrive. So, be sure to do your homework, especially if you're looking to make an impact in different parts of the world. Ultimately, sustainability is about survival. When the market is down or competition is crowding you out, keep going. Show customers what makes you stand out; show them your heart, and you'll soon see the results you want. You want your business to be like the 80-year-old lady who still shows up to yoga every week and stands on her head with the rest of the class. And the only way to do that is through sustainability.

NOTES

NOTES

CHAPTER 10: SCALABILITY

IF YOUR BUSINESS IS SUSTAINABLE, YOU CAN KEEP DOING WHAT YOU'RE DOING FROM NOW until forever. However, if you want your business to grow, it must be flexible, sustainable, *and* scalable. By "scalable," I mean that your business should have the capacity to expand efficiently without being hindered by its current structure or resources. In yoga, you could spend your lifetime running through the same sequence of postures, but most of us want to experience growth and progress. We use simple postures as building blocks for more advanced ones. You might start by perfecting your downward-facing dog, then progress to dolphin pose, and ultimately use those foundations to advance into scorpion pose. One thing leads to another. You're in the flow.

That is unless your practice isn't scalable and you end up toppling over. Every business will experience stumbles, roadblocks, and even failures at some point. My job is to help you avoid them as best as possible. Prevention is the best medicine, after all. Three key objectives will help you build a scalable business: invest in technology and infrastructure, focus on building a strong team, and develop a flexible, adaptable business model. These are the three sides of the triangle of scalability, the three elements you need to maintain balance as your business expands.

Invest in Strong Foundations

As you grow your business, it is important to have the technology and infrastructure in place to support that growth. You wouldn't build a house on a foundation of sand. You want the strongest concrete, steel, and stones you can get! Technology and infrastructure are the foundations of a smoothly running modern business. They increase your company's visibility online, ease day-to-day operations, and smooth out processes with vendors and clients. Technology is a force multiplier when it comes to scaling. You might get by with the basic tools and free options when it's just you and a few clients, but as you grow, you will likely need technology more tailored to your services. It will make your whole operation stronger. Investing in technology may include upgrading your website, implementing new software and tools, and scaling up your hardware and equipment. By making these investments early on, you can avoid bottlenecks and ensure your business can scale efficiently.

When you're smaller, there is time to make decisions as they come. As you look to scale, systematize decisions and operations into repeatable, standardized processes. This will help you consistently deliver services to clients, which is key to scaling. Think of McDonald's. You might think McDonald's sells burgers. Wrong. They sell consistency. (And burgers. Ok, you were right, too.)

You can walk into any franchise in the country, and a Big Mac will be the same in every one. Even more to the point, if you order four Big Mac meals for your family, they will all be identical in quality and taste. McDonald's has consistency nailed. It means customers know what to expect, which generally leads to higher retention rates and brand loyalty. Someone who loves McDonald's fries isn't going to Burger King.

Standardization also makes onboarding easier and more efficient. This is especially true with technology. You want to have standard operating procedures for tracking clients in your CRM, analyzing and applying data, moving clients up the value ladder—everything. As we discussed in Chapter 8, automate as many of your onboarding processes as possible. Many companies have new hires work through training videos and quizzes covering the basics, particularly regarding human resource issues and other standard practices that have to be covered but don't necessarily require person-to-person instruction. Future hires will be able to integrate seamlessly if you systematize.

As you invest in technology and infrastructure, it's important to remember that growth and scaling aren't necessarily synonymous. The most successful ones aren't simply the ones that grow and grow like the Stay Puff Marshmallow Man in *Ghostbusters*. No, the most successful businesses scale by generating increased revenue without adding unnecessary costs along the way. So, before buying the expensive software package with all the bells and whistles, go back to the data. Assess the pain points and where you really need help. Get feedback from your customers on what's working and what could be improved. Go back to our old friend, the SWOT analysis. Then, see what technology will actually benefit you and your team as you scale up.

The A-Team

In yoga, there is a saying: "Be kind to your spine." Every day, it performs the difficult task of keeping you upright in the battle against the force of gravity. It's the central scaffolding of your body. Your team is the backbone of your business, and as you scale, it is important to have a team capable of handling the increased workload.

This means that to avoid bottlenecks as you grow, you want to hire new employees *before* you or your existing team get overloaded. As Jim Collins put it, "First who, then what." In other words, hire the people you need first, then worry about the processes.

For example, if a small business is struggling to get visibility and attract clients despite offering a top-tier service, then the best move might be to create a marketing department. So, the first port of call is hiring a Chief Marketing Officer. They can then help outline the vision for your marketing strategy. Your team can help you go from speaking to a hundred leads to getting one client to a ten-to-one acquisition ratio. Bringing on new talent might mean having to redesign your organizational structure. Take it as an opportunity to think about what structure suits your business best. Should it be flat or hierarchical? Who will report to whom? Do you need different business units for various aspects of your business?

While we're on the subject, I want to briefly loop back to our discussion in Chapter 3 to reiterate just how critical it is to have the *right* people in place. It all comes back to consistency. You don't want to lose that personal touch with customers or risk jeopardizing relationships you've worked hard to cultivate as you built your business from the ground up, nor do you want to dilute your brand. As you bring on new people, you want customers to have the same incredible service and experience as they did before. Having the right team by your side will make all the difference. (And really, who is George Peppard without Mr. T? Come on.)

Another important aspect of building your A-team is to invest in training and development to help your existing team members flourish and take on new responsibilities. You want your team to grow with your business—not outgrow you and move on. If people feel their growth is stagnating while the company skyrockets, they will seek opportunities elsewhere. By offering opportunities for growth and development, you demonstrate to employees that you care and value them. Building a strong team ensures your business can scale without sacrificing quality or customer satisfaction.

Lastly, remember that everyone involved in your operation has an impact. With that in mind, establish solid partnerships with third parties, vendors, or companies with which you can create a joint venture. You don't have to do everything in-house, but you do want to ensure that whatever aspect of the business gets delegated to outside parties is done to your standard. And again, that's where having clear, repeatable processes will make scaling easier.

Strength Through Flexibility

If you found yourself in the middle of a hurricane in Florida, you would see row upon row of palm trees being absolutely blasted by gale-force winds and pummeling rain. What makes these trees so resilient? They're tall, skinny things with barely any branches—you'd think they'd topple right over under that kind of pressure. But palm trees are supported by a flexible midrib that can bend even against the strongest winds. The fronds themselves fold into themselves when they catch a gust of wind, and their flexibility allows the wind to pass over them instead of buckling under the force. While I hope your business never faces a hurricane—literal or metaphorical—it will serve you well to have a business that can stay flexible in the face of adversity.

As your business grows, you may need to pivot or adjust your business model to meet new demands and stay competitive. This requires a willingness to experiment, take risks, and adapt to changing market conditions. By developing a flexible and adaptable business model, you can position your business for long-term growth and success while also being able to respond quickly to new opportunities and challenges. Sometimes, this will be necessary because of external causes. The COVID-19 pandemic is a recent example of businesses needing to be able to weather the proverbial storm. Other times, these causes may be internal.

In my own journey as a solopreneur, I learned this lesson firsthand. When I first started Live Not Loathe, it was targeted at helping men overcome overwhelm. I had only one client in the first six months of business. But then I had a woman inquire. I thought, perhaps now is the time to be more flexible. So I said,

"Sure, I can help." That was the start of my pivot. Three years later, I am pivoting again since my services are now more business-oriented.

And if you're interested in hearing more stories like this, check out my conversation with Founder and CEO of Suzy, Matt Britton, in podcast episode 14 of *Design Your Life & Business*, available anywhere you like to consume your podcasts (e.g., Spotify, Apple Podcasts, YouTube) . We had a fantastic discussion about scaling through partnerships with companies like Google, State Farm, and KPMG (and branding, which we'll discuss in the next chapter). There are some golden nuggets in there about finding inspiration and why every risk you take should be calculated, which is especially true when scaling your business because as the stakes get bigger, your risk/reward threshold changes, too.

Timing Is Everything

The next question many small business owners and entrepreneurs struggle with is when to scale. To this, I would say the better question is: *Why do you want to scale?* Is it for a bigger piece of the pie? To have a greater impact? To increase your bottom line? Maybe you think it's time to take your business global. You must first determine your rationale because if you just scale to scale, you will fail.

Scaling should happen as part of a long-term strategy. For most businesses, the choice to scale comes from a desire to meet a particular revenue goal or because they already have more business than they can handle. A common way of scaling is to add new products and services. If done right, this minimizes your costs while maximizing potential profits.

The AFI framework is a great tool for when you're starting to frame questions about the scalability of your business. AFI, or *analyze, formulate,* and *implement,* links three interdependent strategic management tasks by helping entrepreneurs and stakeholders thoughtfully approach changes to their business or organization. The first step is analyzing your situation. Establish what's happening from a client perspective and an employee perspective. What are your competitive advantages? What resources and capabilities are at your disposal? Then, formulate your business strategy and other functional strategies. This includes looking at what departments you will need to create (marketing, sales, customer service) or what services you might innovate or add to diversify as you grow. Identify what differentiates you from the competition and consider how to convey that to customers. Explore opportunities to partner with other companies with different or bigger capacities as a way to scale. Lastly, what changes might you need to make to organizational structure, company culture, and governance as you implement? Create a plan for how to implement all your brilliant new strategies.

A stakeholder impact analysis is another way to assess whether now is the right time to scale and to help you determine the best way to achieve scale. (You can do this as part of the "Analysis" in your AFI framework.) First, who are your stakeholders, externally and internally? What are they interested in? What opportunities or threats do they present (shout out to SWOT)? What are your economic, social, and governance (ESG) responsibilities to stakeholders? And how do you fully and appropriately address their concerns about scaling?

A lot of people are resistant to change. You might find employees and even customers pushing back against growth. Maybe they like things the way they are or don't understand your vision of growing your business. Or you might discover that there is no demand for the service you want to add. Taking these steps will help you gain alignment with stakeholders early on and ensure the market has the appetite to take on more products and services from you as you begin to scale up.

Perhaps you're thinking, "There's no way I can do this. I run my business, yes, but I don't know how to do all that." Don't panic. It does not necessarily have to be you—the business owner—in charge of scaling. Take Facebook for example. Zuckerberg knew how to code and get people on the platform, but he wasn't that attuned to the business aspect of running a company. Others were more adept in figuring out how to make money from his great idea. Sheryl Sandberg was hired as COO and implemented ad platforms and other changes that made Facebook into the global corporate behemoth it is today. This is just to say it doesn't all have to fall on your shoulders.

Growth is a wonderful thing in all its aspects. I had to do a lot of it to get where I am today, and so did my business. No doubt, like me, you've worked hard to build your business into what it is and have a lot of hope for what it will become. You want the best for it—for your customers, your employees, and yourself. Scaling might seem daunting, but having a flexible business model, your A-team on the ground, and the right technology will help make it a fluid, seamless process. Next, we'll move on to the final "Y" of the 5Y Framework: yearn.

Section Summary:

- Flexibility ensures your business can adapt to changing circumstances.

- Strength in systems and structures creates a resilient foundation.

- Scalability allows your business to grow without being overburdened.

Action Steps:

1. Assess how adaptable your business model is to market changes.

2. Identify one area where your business could become more scalable.

3. Develop a contingency plan for potential disruptions.

4. Invest in employee training to enhance flexibility and innovation within your team.

NOTES

SECTION V: YEARN

By mastering the art of "Yearn," you can build a culture that inspires trust, excitement, and commitment. Loyal customers and engaged employees are the lifeblood of a thriving business, and their enthusiasm fuels organic growth through word-of-mouth referrals and long-term relationships. This chapter provides practical strategies to help you inspire, nurture, and maintain that loyalty, driving your business toward sustainable success.

CHAPTER 11: GENERATING BRAND LOYALTY

YOU MUST HAVE MORE THAN JUST A GREAT PRODUCT OR SERVICE TO ACHIEVE SUCCESS. You must also ensure that customers are filled with so much joy, desire, and confidence in your brand that they become evangelists for it. This is the fifth and final element of the 5Y Framework. You want customers to "yearn" for your brand. There is an undeniable emotional component to customer relationships. A strong emotional bond will build brand loyalty. But how do you accomplish that?

I often hear from clients how much they appreciate my candor. I've shared some of my most personal struggles and successes with you in this book. That's because I think it's important we acknowledge where we've come from and what we've achieved. Truth and honesty are a kind of success in themselves. I struggled with PTSD and depression from my experiences in Afghanistan. That didn't all just disappear when I started coaching. Through therapy, I have learned that every day, you have to decide to win, especially when dealing with mental health issues.

Some days are better than others. Sometimes, I feel the sting of trauma or low mood when I wake up. And I fight it. I say, "That's not me," and I don't let it overcome me. I turn it into an opportunity to reassert myself. It helps me to be transparent about my mental health. Sometimes I talk about it publicly. I can admit days when I feel down, but I refuse to let those feelings derail me from my daily goals and vision. Am I going to let it take me down or fight through it? One thing I know for sure is that I can make that decision to carry on. And the hope is that I might even be able to inspire someone else as a result.

You might find yourself struggling personally or professionally—the chances are high that, as human beings, we're all going to do both. Fighting self-doubt is a big part of entrepreneurship. All business owners doubt themselves sometimes, whether or not they have mental health issues. I remind clients that that's not their voice talking; that's something or someone else. Question where that voice is coming from and in whose interest it is acting.

Find reasons to be great instead of mediocre. Some days, you will feel you aren't performing at your best, and you will feel like throwing in the towel. But you have to find ways to keep yourself from the temptation of succumbing to that mindset. It's not easy. Jocko Willink, an author and leadership instructor, talks about discipline as freedom. Motivation is fleeting. You won't always be motivated; that's a fact. But if you have the discipline to act even when you don't feel motivated, you will accomplish your goals. When I feel I'm lacking motivation, I think of why I started a business in the first place. I remember who I am.

Which brings us to the subject at hand: brand loyalty. As a solopreneur, in many ways, I *am* my brand. So honesty, openness, and relatability are part of my brand and part of what attracts clients to BrightMind Consulting Group. That's one aspect of it, a big one for sure, but a lot goes into developing and distinguishing your brand. So let's break it down. In the following sections, we will cover the essential steps of building a brand: developing your brand identity to define who you are and what you stand for, building relationships to foster trust and loyalty, leveraging storytelling to create emotional connections, and creating feedback loops to adapt and strengthen your brand over time.

Loyalty, Loyalty, Loyalty

Think of Google. Did their logo pop into your mind? Now, imagine working for Google. Are you picturing a sweeping campus with wide, clean walkways, high-tech buildings with ping pong tables, colorful lounges, and free cafes? It's not just a workplace—it's an experience that signals innovation, creativity, and an employee-first culture. This immersive environment reinforces their brand identity and makes them synonymous with forward-thinking solutions and a dynamic work culture.

If you hear, "I'm lovin' it," you think of McDonald's. If you see "Think different," you think of Apple. Major players like these have mastered brand image. And that's because they know that creating a strong brand image is key to brand loyalty. You want to be synonymous with a specific idea that is both bite-sized and big. You want prospects and customers to associate you with a particular solution.

If you want to create brand loyalty, it's essential to have a strong brand image that resonates with your target audience. This means developing a brand identity that's unique, memorable, and consistent across all touchpoints. For example, Wal-Mart is known for "Everyday low prices." Their dominant colors are blue, which signifies trust and security, and yellow, which represents cheerfulness. You won't find them getting into high-end products; their consumers trust them to provide exactly what their brand signals. Likewise, your brand image should communicate your values, mission, and personality in a way that connects with your customers on an emotional level.

While things like colors and logos are important, brand image is more about how you present yourself. So, create a consistent brand message across all channels and ensure that the brand values are reflected in every aspect of the business. What do you want to be known for by your ideal client? What are people saying about you? What are your messaging and taglines conveying? Are they cohesive and consistent?

I don't want people to say, "Jevon is a fantastic consultant," I want them to say, "BrightMind Consulting Group is the premier consulting firm!" Your name is your personal brand; if you're a solopreneur, your name might be stronger than the company name. That's not a bad thing—name recognition is worth celebrating—but in the long term, you want your brand to transcend your name. It means your business can run without your involvement in every aspect. Ideally, you want to be a verb, like Google has become. The name stands for an action that people want.

An easy way to work toward that goal is naming your company something other than your name. Your brand should represent your mission and values, not just the person behind it. Author and online marketing expert Amy Porterfield frames this as switching from a personal brand to a household name. You wouldn't ask someone to hand you a Kimberly-Clark—no way! But a Kleenex is memorable and makes sense. It does what it says on the label.

Brand image is just the first step to building brand loyalty. If you want to attract and retain clients, they need to know more than just your name. You need to build relationships if you want to build brand loyalty. For that, engagement is key. This could include promptly responding to customer inquiries and feedback, offering exclusive content or promotions, and creating a sense of community around your brand. By engaging with your customers, you create a loyal customer base that feels valued and invested in your brand.

I spoke with Alan Weiss, "The Million Dollar Consultant," for my podcast, and he had this to say, "When I went out on my own—and there were 250,000 consultants in the country at that time—I made a couple of decisions that really changed my life. And one was that this is a relationship business; you're selling yourself. And the second is I would never charge for a box of materials or a headcount or a seat or for an hour of time. I would only charge for the value I produced, and those two decisions saved my life."[6]

Alan, like me, is a strong believer in the idea that you should help your clients rather than sell to them. After all, people see sales as adversarial, causing them to stress out and do things they don't want to, which he describes as "a long, slow crawl through enemy territory." Selling frames your relationship as *taking* money from clients, but if you shift your mindset and marketing language to the idea of helping, you're not taking but *giving*. A giving mindset means that when you reach out to clients and prospects, it's to help them out, which reduces friction in the relationship. If you can make this your mindset, you're on the right path, and you'll be better off for it.

Relationship building and engagement must be core to any successful long-term marketing strategy. Customers are savvy, and they come to new brands with a sense of skepticism. They've

---

6 Wooden, Jevon. "Don't Think of a Sale, Think of a Relationship with Alan Weiss, The Million Dollar Consultant." *Design Your Life and Business: The Leaders Podcast.* Podcast audio, 23 August 2023 https://theleaderspod.com/e/286mw33n-dont-think-of-sale-think-of-relationship-alan-weiss-the-million-dollar-consultant

heard every sales pitch from every angle. So again, this is where authenticity is an asset. Don't talk about how great you or your business are; instead, show them how you can help them specifically.

Storytelling is one of the most effective ways to create a strong emotional connection. Stories help customers relate to the brand and create a sense of community and shared values. Use stories throughout your marketing campaigns, social media, and other forms of content marketing to convey why your company can help them survive or thrive. *SPIN-Selling* by Neil Rackham is an excellent resource if you're interested in learning more about this subject in great detail.

Remember also that engagement isn't a one-way street. Be sure that you are listening to your customers and utilizing that feedback. Take time to understand what issues they're having—and sometimes what isn't being said overtly—and realize that every problem is different. Serve their agenda, not your own. Don't downplay or dismiss their fears even if you have encountered their problem many times before. Make every client feel like your number one client. Ultimately, engagement is about service. You create loyal customers who are willing to recommend the brand to others by providing exceptional service.

To that end, it's a good idea to build a circle of referral partners. For example, if you have a customer who you can't serve, either because you don't have the time or capacity or because you think they would be better served elsewhere, have a colleague you can refer them to. Create a network of people you know and trust with whom you can partner to mutually beneficial ends.

Another way to deepen your relationship with customers is to offer personalized experiences. Today's customers expect personalized experiences, and meeting those expectations is crucial to building brand loyalty. By using customer data and insights, you can tailor your marketing efforts and customer interactions to each individual's preferences and needs. This could include personalized product recommendations, targeted marketing campaigns, and personalized customer service.

Get to know customers on a personal level. For instance, use your CRM to gather and store basic client information. Then, use that to build a rapport. Send them a card on their birthday or the one-year anniversary of when they signed up to your email list. (And send it without an "ask"!) Those things stand out and make them feel more than just a name or number, even if they understand it's a marketing strategy. People want to feel seen and appreciated. The key to personalization is to be authentic. Engagement has to be about more than just money. People will see through your efforts if that is the sole motivation. Think of customer communications like a conversation with a friend.

This last one is an oldie but a goodie, the Marvin Gaye or Stevie Wonder of your brand loyalty strategy. Offer rewards and loyalty programs. They are an effective way to incentivize repeat business. By offering exclusive discounts, perks, and rewards for frequent customers, you can create a sense of appreciation and value that encourages customers to return. Loyalty programs can also provide valuable insights into customer behavior and preferences, allowing you to optimize your marketing efforts and improve the customer experience.

For instance, Southwest Airlines is excellent at building customer loyalty through their points program. They offer anniversary points, birthday points, and points for mileage. I use their branded credit card, and Southwest is the first place I go when I book flights. On top of that, their reputation for customer service is well deserved. When they mess up, they own it. When their system went down last year, they gave a ton of points to customers, including those who weren't impacted. I got points, and I wasn't even flying. That's service.

People like loyalty programs because they like perks, sure, but also because it makes them feel valued. There is an emotional component. I try to emulate that through my own loyalty program with giveaways and promotions for repeat clients. There are different models you can play with. I might offer a free service if a customer has spent a certain dollar amount or a referral bonus for clients who stay on for a certain period after referral. The bottom line is to do everything in your power to get people to know who you are and then keep them engaged.

Relationships are powerful tools. They can uplift and motivate us. For example, I met my friend Brooks in basic training. We had a lot in common. We both had tough upbringings and were on this path of seeking change for our families. Brooks was from Memphis and had a baby girl back home who was his world. We became fast friends, and when I injured my ankle, he pushed me to stay strong and keep going. When I felt down, he picked me up. We even managed to "liberate" a cell phone from the drill sergeant and stashed it in an empty deodorant stick so we could call our families.

Brooks became like a brother to me. We talked about everything—what it was like to be away from home for the first time in our lives, how much it meant to be able to speak to our families or send letters home, and what we wanted for our futures.

Business, like basic training, shouldn't be a lonely journey. Building brand loyalty, cultivating relationships, and growing your network means success, yes, *and* they mean you can run your business joyfully and alongside people who share your vision.

Loop It Back

The other major facet of building brand loyalty is creating feedback loops. What do I mean by that? Essentially, it is the process of using customer or employee feedback to improve your products or services or make the workplace a happier, better space for employees. It's a process of refinement. Listening to and using customer feedback to improve the product or service is a low-cost way to show them that their opinions are valued and helps your business stay top of mind.

The first step in creating a feedback loop is soliciting feedback from customers regularly to understand their needs and pain points. One effective way is by sending out surveys or feedback forms after they make a purchase or use a service. It is essential to keep the questions simple, specific, and open-ended to gather more detailed information about their experience. You can also conduct focus groups, online forums, or social media polls to gather more in-depth feedback and identify areas for improvement.

Then, put it to good use! Analyzing customer feedback provides valuable insights into what customers like and dislike about your products or services. It can help identify features that need improvement or additional functionalities that customers might need. By addressing customer needs and concerns, you can improve customer satisfaction and loyalty while boosting sales. The point is to initiate change through knowledge.

We've talked about processes and automation, so you should be able to guess the next step. Implement a system for responding to customer feedback promptly and effectively. It is crucial that you respond in a timely manner, whether the feedback is positive or negative. Your response shows customers that their opinions are valued and that the business is actively working to improve their experience. Consider automating feedback responses to ensure customers receive prompt responses and follow up with them to ensure their concerns are addressed.

We all have inboxes full of requests to review purchases and services. How many do you respond to? Your business needs feedback, and a good way to get more of it is to offer incentives like discounts or free products. Customers are more likely to provide feedback if there is a benefit to them. Incentives encourage customers to provide more detailed and honest feedback. It also helps build customer loyalty and retention by keeping the line open and the conversation going.

Last but most importantly, use it! The point of customer feedback is to identify areas for improvement in customer service, product development, and marketing. If you don't use it, you may as well not ask for it in the first place. In contrast, regularly reviewing customer feedback can help identify trends, issues, or opportunities that you can take advantage of. It can provide insights into new product features, marketing campaigns, or customer service improvements. Using customer feedback to improve different aspects of your business can lead to more significant revenue growth, improved customer satisfaction, and a more competitive edge.

Listening to your customers and showing them that you hear them builds trust, credibility, and loyalty. And brand loyalty is a vital source of growth for your business. It's a pool of customers you can rely on because they feel they can rely on you. The more seeds you plant, the more flowers you'll see grow.

NOTES

NOTES

CHAPTER 12: MARKETING

FEW OF US HAVE MILLION-DOLLAR AD BUDGETS, BUT I'LL LET YOU IN ON A SECRET: WE don't need them. You can avoid spending tens of thousands of dollars on paid ads by employing organic marketing strategies.

In contrast to paid advertising, which involves explicitly paying to place content in front of your target audience, organic marketing is all about attracting your audience naturally over time, typically through social media engagement, search engine results, and word-of-mouth. Organic marketing has the added benefit of appearing less intrusive to prospects and customers, and it's more cost-effective, which makes it more sustainable as a long-term strategy. So, what can you do to leverage organic marketing?

In the context of organic marketing, relationships are the most important currency. The customer relationships you foster underscore your reputation, word-of-mouth referrals, and, ultimately, business growth. You can also benefit your partners and affiliates by complementing their services with your own—and vice versa—increasing the value of both. We'll look at a few of the key relationships you need for successful organic marketing.

You Down with OPP?

In this case, OPP is "Other People's Platforms," and if you're not down with them already, you should be. One of the most efficient, cost-effective ways to boost your brand visibility is simply to borrow someone else's. Now, this covers a lot of ground, so I'll walk you through all the ways you can leverage other people's platforms to gain access to a wider audience—without the hard work of having to get butts in the seats yourself.

Thought Leadership

No, I'm not saying you should start a cult. Thought leadership just means demonstrating that you're an expert in your corner of the business world, and it's a great way to reach a wide and varied audience. Establishing yourself as a thought leader in your industry can attract a steady stream of quality leads. Share your expertise through public speaking engagements, webinars, podcasts, and guest blogging on authoritative platforms. By providing valuable insights and solutions to industry challenges, you'll position yourself as a trusted authority, leading to increased visibility, credibility, and organic lead generation. I use a mix of these in my own business.

When it comes to speaking engagements, I focus on professional service firms and agencies. Chambers of Commerce and speakers' associations are always looking for engaging presenters. People think it's hard to land these gigs. It's not. It can be as simple as reaching out to the organizer, pitching a topic relevant to them, and giving a strong presentation. You are likely to be invited back or to give a workshop. For example, I organized a workshop on lead generation for Houston's East End Chamber of Commerce. That puts me directly in front of prospective clients and gives me the opportunity to build a name for myself locally—while providing useful content to the audience. And there's an association for just about every industry out there.

Podcasting is also a popular medium for thought leaders to promote themselves. They have become increasingly popular in recent years, and many people rely on them as a source of entertainment, information, and inspiration. That said, the podcast field is saturated, and it usually takes years to build up a following. Rather than starting your own, I suggest being a guest on established podcasts. Appearing on podcasts instantly boosts your credibility as an authority in your field. I host *Design Your Life and Business*, but I've also appeared on hundreds of podcasts: *Million Dollar Mastermind*, *Boss Uncaged*, *Dream Business Radio*, and the list goes on.

Look up the top podcasts in your industry and pitch them on your story. Before you approach a podcast host or producer, it's essential to understand the show's content, tone, and format. This will help you tailor your pitch to the specific interests and needs of the podcast and increase your chances of being selected as a guest. Do your homework. Listen to episodes, read the show notes, and check out their website and social media profiles. Once you have a feel for the show's style, pitch them by highlighting your unique insights, showcasing your experience and qualifications, and explaining why you would be a valuable guest. In the military, we say, "Bottom line up front," or in other words, be straight and to the point. Be confident and concise and follow up if you haven't heard back after a week or two.

Hopefully, you do land a spot. So be sure to prepare! Don't throw away your shot. Most podcast hosts ask beforehand what questions you'd like to be asked. Take the opportunity to set yourself up: have them ask questions that will let you connect with listeners. Have your one-sheet ready.

And remember that podcasting is a long game; you might not garner immediate results. That said, it does provide a searchable record of your expertise or viewpoint, giving current prospects the chance to search for you. You can add backlinks to your website, boosting your site's reputation score. You might even consider using the transcript of your appearance and parlaying it into a blog, which brings us to our next OPP-ortunity: blogging.

It might seem "old-fashioned" to some, but blogs still hold a certain amount of prestige, and they can be highly effective for communicating more complex ideas. Guest blogging for the likes of *Forbes* or *Fast Company* will bolster your reputation as a thought leader and garner thousands of readers (*and* a backlink to your website). Many times, depending on the terms of your agreement, you can also repost your article to your own site.

One of my most impactful blogs was written for the *Houston Business Journal*. It had an even greater impact on my brand visibility than I'd had writing for bigger publications. This is to say, as with everything you do as part of an organic marketing strategy, you want to target guest blogs where your ideal clients congregate.

And lastly, television spots are another great organic marketing opportunity. I was recently on ABC News here in Houston, speaking about the impact of helping minorities gain equity (access to capital) *and* mentorship. I got to speak about my work as a business coach and how we can address the lack of opportunities for minority business owners. I happen to be friends with a reporter at the station affiliate. We met at a cooking class, and I was able to leverage that relationship for a TV appearance. It helps to talk to everyone all the time. You never know when an opportunity will emerge.

This kind of marketing is a two-way street. The people running these platforms need contributors, and we need opportunities. It's a win-win.

Influencer Marketing

We are influencers whether we like it or not. We are all being looked at, or up to, by someone. Collaborating with influencers and industry thought leaders who align with your brand values can be a game-changer for lead generation. Influencers have cultivated trust and authority among their followers, making their recommendations highly potent. By leveraging their reach and engaging them in partnerships, you can tap into their audience and generate quality leads who are more likely to convert into customers.

That said, I don't pay for influencers or give away free services, and I don't suggest you do that either unless you've really done the homework to ensure their audience takes buying actions from their content. You might as well pay for an ad if you're going to pay an influencer. Instead, I look for people I can collaborate with, people with convening interests. I reach out and see what they want. For example, if they have a course coming out soon, I will say, "I'd love to have a conversation about how I can help you." Then, I can promote their course via my email list or invite them to speak on my podcast. The key is to create mutually beneficial relationships that can be leveraged for free.

Start by conducting research and identifying relevant influencers in your industry or niche. Their mission and values should align with your own. You also want to consider factors such as the size of their following, engagement rate, and audience demographics to determine if they are a good fit for your business.

I discussed this with Hannah Acosta, social media manager at Ugly Mug Marketing, on an episode of *Design Your Life and Business*.7 Hannah is a passionate and purposeful leader who has grown her department by over 340 percent in the last four years. She has worked alongside hundreds of small business owners and entrepreneurs as they navigate the ever-changing digital marketing landscape. Hannah noted that some of her clients struggled to identify their target audience at first. Sometimes, Hannah said, it's as simple as noticing who is buying from you, who is coming into your store, who is calling and emailing you. With that data, you can put together an avatar to show who your

---

7 Wooden, Jevon. "How to Build a Social Media Strategy with Hannah Acosta, Social Media Manager at Ugly Mug Marketing." *Design Your Life and Business: The Leaders Podcast.* Podcast audio, 22 August 2023 https://theleaderspod.com/e/0nj2vw5n-how-to-build-a-social-media-strategy-with-hannah-acosta

typical customer is and use it to ease the targeting process of digital marketing.

It's not just about having thousands of followers. It's about the value you're adding to your business. In a world inundated with influencers, how do you know who to partner with? The question I always start with is, "Where does your ideal client congregate?" Your ideal client likely frequents one or two channels, so concentrate your efforts there. Don't spread yourself thin by trying to have a presence everywhere. You want quality over quantity.

Once you have identified potential influencers, reach out to them and introduce yourself and your brand. Offer to collaborate with them on a campaign or project and be clear about your expectations and goals for the partnership. Like any relationship, it should be balanced, and it's ok to set boundaries to protect your interests and those of your customers.

Then, let the collaboration begin. Work with the influencer to create content that showcases your product or service in an authentic and engaging way. This could include sponsored posts on social media, blog posts, or product reviews. Be sure to disclose the sponsored nature of the content to comply with FTC guidelines. You can also use that influencer-generated content on your own social media channels and website to increase visibility and reach. This will reinforce your partnership with the influencer and build credibility with your audience.

And, of course, data is king. Every partnership is, in some ways, an experiment. To know which influencer partnerships are really serving your business, you need to track and measure the success of influencer campaigns. Use analytics tools, like the ones discussed in Chapter 4, to monitor their success in terms of engagement, reach, and sales. I like to use the old-school method. Look at their posts, note their data, and have them send you the insights. A post on social media has a short timeline, maybe a couple of hours before you generate results. LinkedIn is longer, anywhere from two to twenty-four hours, before you get data on its impact. Use this information to refine your influencer marketing strategy and optimize future campaigns.

You can use roughly this same model to build an affiliate marketing strategy. The primary difference will be that you need to develop clear and enticing commission structures for affiliates and empower them with the tools and resources to effectively promote products or services. It's one more avenue for getting your brand out there in front of the right people.

Keeping It Old School

"Yearn" is all about getting clients to talk about how awesome you are. And word-of-mouth remains one of the most effective forms of marketing. There are a number of ways to do this effectively, efficiently, and with little or no cost to your business.

Encourage satisfied customers to share their positive experiences with friends and family. You can do this through email campaigns, social media, or in-person conversations. Social media platforms offer immense potential for reaching and engaging with your target audience organically. You can create meaningful connections, share valuable content, and foster an online community around your brand. Interact with customers on social media by responding to comments and messages, sharing user-generated content, and hosting contests or giveaways. You can even create content for followers to share with others. This helps build a community of loyal customers who feel connected to your brand.

When it comes to following trends on social media, Hannah pointed out that it is not about simply going with whatever is popular.[8] Study the current trends and figure out what suits you and your company as a brand. Check in with similar businesses or competitors to see if they are jumping on the trend. If they are, is it working for them? Do your research, and don't just thoughtlessly follow every single trend. That won't win you positive results.

Referrals are the bread and butter of word-of-mouth marketing. Incentivize current customers to refer new customers by offering referral rewards or discounts. This not only encourages repeat business but also expands your customer base. By implementing a referral program, you can tap into your existing network of satisfied customers to generate quality leads. This organic approach generates high-quality leads and builds trust and credibility for your brand.

Providing exceptional customer service that exceeds expectations and leaves a lasting impression is another way to get people talking about your brand. This can include personalized interactions, resolving issues quickly and efficiently, and offering unexpected perks or rewards. When I have a positive experience—

---

8 Ibid.

whether at a shop or restaurant, a garage, getting repairs done on my house, whatever it is—I go out of my way to share that experience with people I know. If your business consistently goes above and beyond to provide outstanding customer service that creates a positive experience for your customers, you'll find they will become your greatest cheerleaders.

As you engage with prospects and customers online, be sure to monitor reviews and respond to any negative feedback in a positive and helpful manner. You want responses to show that you care about the customer's experience and are willing to make things right. This not only helps address any issues but also shows potential customers that you value customer satisfaction. You can turn that "threat" into an "opportunity" if you stay on top of your online ratings.

Reuse, Recycle, Repurpose

Making content with OPP is invaluable to growing your profile and amping up your business, but we must still produce content on our platforms. Content marketing is a potent tool for establishing credibility, building trust, and generating leads organically. By creating high-quality, informative, and engaging content, you can attract your target audience and position yourself as an industry expert. From insightful blog posts and informative videos to in-depth whitepapers and case studies, producing valuable content tailored to your audience's needs will drive organic traffic and generate leads.

If you're unsure where to start, Hannah Acosta suggests starting small and setting goals. "We can't be everywhere at all times, and so, when we get on these platforms, it's important for us to set a goal. It's ok if our big-picture goal at the end of the year is to be posting once a day, but for now, what's realistic is to be posting twice a week. We need to set our goal so we can manage our expectations and not be too hard on ourselves."[9]

I always suggest that clients repurpose everything they can. I do this myself, too. If I create a video to post on LinkedIn, you are going to see it a week later on my website, Facebook, and other platforms. There is one caveat to this, however, because you want to keep your content fresh. Pick one primary platform to focus on. For me, that's LinkedIn. LinkedIn favors long-form content, so when I do want to repost content on other sites, I tailor it accordingly.

I generally like to have five "buckets" or categories for each topic I create content for. Each piece of content will fit in one of these buckets, and within each bucket, I have five sub-buckets. Is that too much? No, absolutely not. What does this look like in practice? Say I'm discussing leadership; that's one bucket. But that's quite broad. So, I would break that into sub-buckets on leadership relating to conflict resolution, effective communication, authenticity, culture, and delegation. This encourages you to stake out a niche instead of trying to cover everything in one go. It also makes it easy to plan out content marketing for the next year since you have a ready-made list of topics to draw from.

It can feel overwhelming to create your own content if it's not your area of expertise. However, a few simple dos and don'ts

---

9 Ibid.

can help you navigate this process. *Don't* force your service or product down someone's throat; avoid the hard sell. People don't respond well to that kind of pressure. And *don't* push your product on people who have given no indication they are interested. That's also why it's so important to know who your ideal client is and where to find them. *Don't* blast prospects with a wall of text. Whether we like it or not, our attention spans have shrunk. So be concise and make every word count! And lastly, *don't* look to be everywhere. Select where you need to be based on the data and research and invest your resources accordingly. This isn't static either; you might find your primary platform and audience shifts over time.

Do promote yourself. Let people know you are here to help. Be consistent with your posts; schedule them for the same time or day each week. *Do* make your content fun and engaging; use images or videos to convey or emphasize some of your ideas. Be creative. *Do* repurpose content. Convert blogs to video to podcast episodes. You can even republish content from six months earlier if you're short of time or ideas. Squeeze all the juice out of that fruit.

Shifting the focus toward organic marketing and nurturing customer relationships is no longer just an option for service-based businesses. It's a necessity for long-term success. Developing innovative and efficient organic marketing strategies is sure to land you remarkable outcomes without breaking the bank. Remember, the strength of your business lies in the power of the relationships you build. Be authentic, be engaging, and most importantly, be there for your customers and partners.

With these strategies, you're not just building a business but a community.

Summary:

- Passionate customers and employees drive organic growth through advocacy.

- Fostering loyalty requires a deep understanding of your audience's needs and aspirations.

- Creating a culture of trust and excitement fuels enthusiasm for your brand.

Action Steps:

1. Conduct a survey or gather feedback from customers to identify areas for improvement.

2. Develop a plan to strengthen employee engagement and satisfaction.

3. Create a loyalty program or incentive to reward repeat customers.

4. Share your brand's mission and values through storytelling to inspire deeper connections.

NOTES

CONCLUSION: IMPLEMENTING THE 5Y FRAMEWORK

HERE WE ARE. WE'VE REACHED THE CONCLUSION OF THE 5Y FRAMEWORK AND COVERED A lot of ground along the way. Our journey began with the humble yardstick: learning to set realizable goals, measuring success, and differentiating from competitors. We then progressed to yield and uncovered what levers you can pull to maximize your potential, especially through your people and technology. In the third part of the framework, we discussed yare and how you can make your life easier with the three Ds—delegation, deletion, and delaying—and through automation. It's the 21st century, after all! With those pieces in place, we moved on to yoga and how to design your business so it is flexible, sustainable, and scalable enough to weather any storm and grow well into the future. And lastly, we shared ideas on yearn: how to make your customers the best advertisers for your brand by generating brand loyalty and implementing impactful organic marketing strategies.

To give you one more look at what integrating the 5Y Framework can do to invigorate your business, let's return to our friend, the electrician. Tad had been running his business for 20 years. It was all he knew. He'd built it from the ground up and had as many as 20 employees on staff. But the business was ailing. They were struggling to attract new customers and retain existing clients. He had employees to pay, bills to pay, and his own retirement to look after. He turned to me as a coach for help.

Website traffic was down, and the company was getting poor reviews. Within the 5Y Framework, their primary yardstick was to increase customer acquisition and retention.

Next, we looked at yield. When it came to the people component of the business, we found that everyone on staff was doing multiple jobs. They were spread thin, and people were responsible for tasks they didn't have the talent for or weren't interested in. We had to make the employees more specialized. We created different departments for sales, customer service, and technicians and hired an independent contractor to handle their social media.

Technologically, they weren't tracking anything. There was no feedback system for gauging and responding to customer complaints. They didn't even have a CRM to keep track of when customers had what work done or when they were due for further maintenance. We set up a CRM along with automated emails so customers knew exactly when maintenance was due and when technicians were coming out for regularly scheduled visits. We integrated the system with Google Maps so customers could track technicians in real-time and call them if needed. That helped with retention and success.

To assess their needs for yield, I conducted an analysis of their digital presence to get an impression of why they were struggling with acquisition. I found that they had no online presence. They weren't on Yelp. Their Facebook page was woefully out of date.

And their attempts at SEO were a mess. Our social media consultant built up their online presence, and I helped them create content. We started posting twice a day on Facebook and Instagram and three times daily on LinkedIn to bolster their digital presence. We also retooled their SEO with a local emphasis so customers could find them and removed dead links to further elevate their SEO.

The yare here has some overlaps because the levers we pulled for yield made things easier for people by default. Decisions like splitting staff into departments made it easier for people to specialize, and the CRM helped automate customer communication. For their website, we also added a chatbot to answer quick questions on a 24/7 basis. It could answer simple questions and book appointments around the clock, which made it easier for customers to get what they needed without the wait.

As for yoga, Tad knew he needed to expand operations if he wanted to compete. His original location was in a suburb northwest of Houston. Houston proper has many electrician services firms, but the outskirts tend to be underserved. So, he decided to open another location in the southeast corner of the city. I helped him find low-cost leases for warehouses and directed him toward low-interest loans available to veterans.

Now, Tad's biggest issue had been customer acquisition and retention. When it came to the yearn factor, I knew we needed to get more customers to leave reviews for Tad's business. They provided great service and quality workmanship, but no one was spreading the word because, well, there was nowhere to do it. As part of the CRM, we set up email requests for feedback. Once a technician marks a job complete in the system, a request goes out automatically to customers so they can rate them on Google or Yelp right away. We also went back and checked in with past and lapsed clients. In the winter of 2021, there were major outages in Texas, so Tad's company offered select customers free maintenance calls to refresh those relationships. And by selling generators, you create a client relationship for life.

Meanwhile, we set up brand ambassadors—mostly the technicians, electricians, and generator maintenance people—who record content while working and sometimes take photos with happy clients. These get posted to social media and reinforce their brand image as a small, local company that provides top-notch service. We even got a local news station to do a story on the business. All these measures create momentum, and that momentum snowballs into something great. And now they're doing better than they ever have.

These are the stories and experiences that make me proud to be a coach. The fulfillment I gain from helping others succeed keeps me going. I had to overcome a very dark period en route to slaying my demons and succeeding as a small business owner. I lost my way after my deployment. It took time for me to learn the strength of vulnerability. I wouldn't be here today if not for that lesson, which hit me hardest when I was at my lowest.

In September 2017, about six months after returning home from Afghanistan, I was in a very bleak place. I was lying on the couch in my apartment in Bloomfield, New Jersey. I was struggling with PTSD, loneliness, disconnection, and purposelessness. I was directionless. I was in a bad place. The lights were off.

The television was off. I was just lying there in the dark, thinking about a world without me in it. I picked up the phone to call my sister—a last-ditch effort.

"I'm sorry," I said. "I just don't want to do this anymore."

She just listened. She didn't interrupt me. For me, I felt like what happened in Afghanistan was *still happening*. PTSD impacts us because we don't associate a time period with an event. Our body responds to a threat that no longer exists, treating memories as present dangers. I was living through the base bombing over and over, even though it was in the distant past. My mind and body were trapped in a cycle of re-experiencing the trauma, unable to recognize that I was safe and far removed from that moment.

"Get help," she said when I had finished.

At that time, I didn't know I *could* get help. This one insight has blessed me more than I can ever tell. It was a kind of rebirth for me. A renewal. An epiphany.

That lesson enabled me to become a coach. I recognized that I didn't have all my ducks in a row, that things weren't as perfect as I was pretending, and that I needed help. The 5Y Framework is about being vulnerable, recognizing you can't do everything and don't have all the resources. You don't have to say you're ok when you're not. Openness allowed me to become a coach and a business leader, whereas being closed off almost cost me my life and my business. And I've come out the other side bigger and better.

Whatever it is you're struggling with—whether it's PTSD or generating consistent revenue—there is help. And the future is bright. The path is in front of you; you just have to take the first step. Start by setting your goals and working your way through the 5Y Framework.

One thing I find myself saying more and more to clients is to take a step back. We're leaning too much on ads and technology and missing out on human connections, empathy, and leadership. We have to put ourselves back in the shoes of the customer. We must think deeply about their needs and how to establish a long-term relationship. Each person you serve has a lifetime value for your business.

Get back to the core of what your business is. You can't be all things to all people. Develop the profile of your ideal client so you can better target them for acquisition. How can you simplify your service offerings and remove friction for clients who want to work with you? Think about what kind of value ladder you're offering customers and how you deliver services. Find the levers to pull to get people to evangelize for you and advance your organic marketing strategy. And be mindful of your digital persona and presence; take ownership of your online content and profiles.

I wrote this book as a guide you can refer back to many times as your business evolves. The framework is not necessarily linear. You might find different aspects more relevant at different times and phases in your business. So *do* perform a self-check diagnostic multiple times throughout the year. Business moves quickly. New technology emerges. It's a dynamic landscape. You have to constantly adapt to those changes.

As for me, I'm also adapting to big changes. At the time of writing this book, my first child, a baby girl, Jevonne Ceylon Wooden, is soon to be born. My driving goal is to leverage my business to get more time to spend with family on what matters most. That, truly, is more important than money. I hope to travel more, do more speaking engagements, and give back more. I would like to expand my work with prisons and youth. I plan to establish a nonprofit program to give back more to marginalized communities, help grow their businesses, and work with struggling entrepreneurs to generate their first $100k in business.

And as for my PTSD, it still sometimes raises its ugly head. Each year, on Veterans Day, I take time to shed tears and reflect. Each year, I read the article about the bombing and try to ground myself. I try to stay humble, thankful, and, most of all, grateful. I remind myself and others that while life feels long sometimes, it is actually short. We don't know when that time is going to come. We must make the most of it. Make sure you live a life of service, a life that is full. Don't waste time doing something that drags you down. Do something that invigorates you. Don't stay in the hurt, personally or professionally. Figure out how to make circumstances better for yourself and those around you. You always have that power.

5Y FRAMEWORK *CASE STUDY* — ALEX: SaaS

Alex is the founder of GrowthHub, a SaaS platform that helps small businesses track and optimize their customer acquisition strategies. Despite building a useful product, Alex struggled to grow the business. Revenue was inconsistent, customer retention was a challenge, and Alex found it difficult to balance product development with business growth. Feeling overwhelmed, Alex decided to apply the 5Y Framework to transform both the leadership approach and the company's operations.

Y A R D S T I C K

STEP 1

DEFINING SUCCESS

Alex started by clearly defining what success looked like for GrowthHub:

- Achieve $1 million in annual recurring revenue (ARR) within 18 months.
- Reduce churn rate from 15% to under 5%.
- Onboard 50 new customers per month, focusing on medium-sized businesses in the tech and retail industries.

Alex also set measurable KPIs, such as increasing customer lifetime value (CLV) by 25% and improving onboarding time by 50%. With these goals in place, the team had a clear direction for the company's growth.

STEP 2

CREATING A PLAN TO HIT THE GOAL

To achieve these goals, Alex created a step-by-step strategy:

- **Focus on Core Features:** Instead of building new features, Alex prioritized improving the platform's user experience and refining the top three features customers loved most.
- **Strengthen Customer Support:** Alex expanded the customer success team to proactively engage with users, answer questions, and reduce churn.
- **Targeted Marketing:** GrowthHub shifted from broad marketing to hyper-focused campaigns targeting tech and retail businesses. This included hosting webinars and creating case studies to showcase the platform's ROI.

Every action the team took was tied directly to improving the metrics that mattered most.

STEP 3

SIMPLIFYING PROCESSES

Alex realized that many internal processes were slowing the company down. Applying "yare" (ease and simplicity), Alex streamlined operations:

- **Automated Onboarding:** The company invested in an in-app onboarding process that guided new users through setup without requiring human intervention.
- **Simplified Pricing:** GrowthHub moved from a complex pricing model to three clear tiers, making it easier for customers to choose the right plan.
- **Internal Communication Tools:** Alex implemented Slack and project management tools like Notion to improve team communication and reduce time wasted on unnecessary meetings.

These changes made the business more agile and reduced inefficiencies, giving Alex more time to focus on strategy.

BUILDING FLEXIBILITY AND STRENGTH

To ensure GrowthHub could thrive in a competitive SaaS market, Alex focused on making the company flexible and resilient:

- Predictable Revenue Streams: Alex introduced an annual subscription discount, which encouraged customers to commit longer-term, stabilizing cash flow.
- Upselling Opportunities: GrowthHub added premium features for enterprise users, creating a scalable revenue stream.
- Scenario Planning: Alex worked with the team to develop contingency plans for potential challenges, such as economic downturns or increased competition.

By creating a strong foundation and scalable structure, Alex ensured that GrowthHub was prepared for sustainable growth.

INSPIRING LOYALTY AND ADVOCACY

Alex focused on turning GrowthHub's customers into enthusiastic advocates for the platform:

- Customer Feedback Loops: The team implemented a Net Promoter Score (NPS) survey to regularly gather customer insights and act on feedback.
- Exclusive Community: Alex launched a private Slack group where customers could network, share tips, and provide feedback on GrowthHub's roadmap.
- Content Marketing: GrowthHub shared success stories of customers who had dramatically improved their ROI using the platform, inspiring trust and excitement.

These efforts helped create a loyal customer base that frequently referred new users and advocated for GrowthHub in their industries.

RESULTS

RESULTS OF APPLYING THE 5Y FRAMEWORK

By implementing the 5Y Framework, Alex transformed GrowthHub into a thriving SaaS company:

- Revenue Growth: GrowthHub reached $1.2 million ARR within 14 months.
- Customer Retention: The churn rate dropped to 4%, thanks to a better onboarding process and proactive customer success efforts.
- New Customer Acquisition: GrowthHub consistently onboarded 60 new customers per month, exceeding the original goal.
- Team Productivity: Streamlined processes improved efficiency, allowing the team to focus on growth rather than putting out fires.
- Customer Advocacy: Over 30% of new customers came from referrals, reducing the company's acquisition costs and building a strong brand reputation.

YOUR TURN

Just like Alex, you can use the 5Y Framework to tackle your biggest challenges and achieve extraordinary results. Whether you're running a SaaS company, a consultancy, or another type of business, the principles of Yardstick, Yield, Yare, Yoga, and Yearn are universally applicable. Take the first step today: define your yardstick, map out your goals, and start transforming your leadership and business from functional to phenomenal. Your journey to success begins now!

5Y FRAMEWORK *CASE STUDY* SARAH:CONSULTING

Sarah is the owner of a small marketing consultancy that specializes in helping local businesses improve their branding and social media presence. Despite being passionate about her work and having loyal clients, Sarah found herself stuck in a cycle of constant hustle without meaningful growth. She felt overwhelmed, unsure of how to scale her business, and frustrated by inconsistent revenue. That's when she decided to apply the 5Y Framework to transform her leadership and business.

Y A R D S T I C K — STEP 1

DEFINING SUCCESS

Sarah started by clearly defining her goals. She realized that her previous measures of success (just paying the bills and keeping clients happy) were too vague and didn't motivate her. She redefined her yardstick to include:

- Generating $200,000 in annual revenue.
- Hiring a part-time assistant to free up her time.
- Expanding her client base to include medium-sized businesses with larger budgets.

By setting measurable KPIs, such as signing three new clients every quarter and increasing her average client retainer by 30%, Sarah had a clear destination for her business.

YIELD — STEP 2

CREATING A PLAN TO HIT THE GOAL

With her goals in place, Sarah mapped out a step-by-step strategy to achieve them:

- Streamlining Services: She reduced her service offerings to focus on her most profitable packages, such as comprehensive branding strategies.
- Pricing Adjustments: She increased her rates to reflect the value of her expertise, ensuring her business remained sustainable while attracting high-quality clients.
- Client Acquisition: Sarah implemented a referral program and hosted free branding workshops to showcase her expertise and attract ideal clients.

Her plan ensured that every action she took contributed directly to her overall goals.

STEP 3

SIMPLIFYING PROCESSES

Sarah realized that her day-to-day operations were unnecessarily complicated. She applied "yare" (ease and simplicity) to her business by:

- Automating Repetitive Tasks: Using tools like Asana for project management and QuickBooks for invoicing saved her hours each week.
- Delegating Work: She hired a part-time virtual assistant to handle administrative tasks, allowing her to focus on strategy and client relationships.
- Creating Standard Operating Procedures (SOPs): Sarah documented her workflows so that future team members could onboard seamlessly and maintain consistent quality.

These changes made her business more efficient and gave her the mental bandwidth to focus on growth.

BUILDING FLEXIBILITY AND STRENGTH

To future-proof her business, Sarah worked on making her consultancy both flexible and resilient:

- **Diversifying Revenue Streams:** She created an online course teaching small business owners the basics of branding. This provided passive income and reduced her dependence on one-on-one client work.
- **Building Resilience:** She saved a portion of her profits to create a financial cushion, ensuring her business could weather lean months.
- **Scaling Smartly:** By optimizing her services and creating scalable products, Sarah positioned her business to grow sustainably without overextending herself.

These steps ensured that Sarah's business could thrive, even in a competitive and unpredictable market.

INSPIRING LOYALTY AND ADVOCACY

Finally, Sarah focused on turning her clients and team into enthusiastic advocates for her brand:

- **Delighting Clients:** She provided personalized touches, such as custom thank-you notes and surprise add-ons, which left her clients feeling valued and appreciated.
- **Building Relationships:** Sarah created a private Facebook group for her clients to share success stories, ask questions, and connect with her directly.
- **Storytelling:** She shared her own journey and client success stories on social media, which helped build an emotional connection with her audience and attract more referrals.

These efforts created a loyal community of clients who regularly referred her services to others and actively promoted her brand.

RESULTS OF APPLYING THE 5Y FRAMEWORK

Within 12 months, Sarah had transformed her business:

- She exceeded her revenue goal, generating $250,000 in annual income.
- She signed six new high-value clients through her workshops and referrals.
- Her online course brought in an additional $30,000 in passive income.
- Her business ran more smoothly than ever, thanks to streamlined processes and a part-time assistant.

Most importantly, Sarah felt energized and confident, knowing she had built a business she loved that aligned with her goals and values.

YOUR TURN

Like Sarah, you have the power to transform your leadership and business from functional to phenomenal. The 5Y Framework isn't just a concept—it's a practical, actionable roadmap for success. Take the first step today by defining your yardstick and setting your sights on the phenomenal future you want to create. Your transformation starts now!

ABOUT THE AUTHOR

I AM JEVON WOODEN, A LEADERSHIP AND BUSINESS COACH, SPEAKER, AUTHOR, AND US Army veteran. My journey to becoming a leadership and personal development expert has been shaped by personal adversity, relentless determination, and the desire to help others rise above their challenges. I have faced numerous obstacles throughout my life, but each experience made me stronger, more insightful, and deeply committed to empowering others to achieve their full potential.

My path to leadership expertise is rooted in resilience and emotional intelligence, which I discovered and honed through personal and professional experiences. These formative lessons laid the groundwork for my success in the military and later in the business world. During my military career, I led with integrity and courage, earning the prestigious Bronze Star for my leadership during a bombing attack at Bagram Air Base in Afghanistan. This harrowing experience solidified my belief in leading with empathy and understanding, values that I now share with leaders and organizations around the world.

Transitioning from the military, I found my passion in coaching and consulting, applying my principles of empathetic leadership to help businesses and individuals reach new heights. My approach is simple yet powerful: I believe that empathetic leadership is the key to fostering high-performing teams, cultivating innovation, and boosting employee engagement. By integrating data-driven strategies with a deep understanding of human behavior, I empower leaders to unlock the full potential of their teams and achieve sustainable growth.

I have also had the privilege of working with Verizon Small Business Digital Ready, supporting entrepreneurs across the nation in growing and scaling their businesses. This experience further fueled my passion for helping business leaders navigate challenges and seize opportunities for success.

I am incredibly passionate about marketing and sales and guiding motivated individuals and organizations to reach their goals. My coaching and consulting services span leadership development, performance improvement, change management, and team dynamics. Clients trust me to break down complex concepts into actionable strategies that lead to real, measurable success. I draw on my military discipline, business acumen, and unwavering belief in empathetic leadership to inspire change and growth.

My thought leadership has earned recognition in respected publications such as *Forbes, Entrepreneur*, and *Inc. Magazine*, where I share insights on leadership, business growth, and the power of emotional intelligence in today's fast-paced world. Beyond my professional achievements, I'm committed to giving back to the community and mentoring future leaders. I actively engage in speaking engagements, workshops, and one-on-one coaching sessions to inspire and support others in overcoming their own challenges.

If you're interested in learning more about the 5Y Framework or other topics from this book, I invite you to visit my website FunctionalToPhenomenal.com, where you can sign up for newsletters, subscribe to my podcast, and connect with me. Let's keep the conversation going and build a world where leaders thrive, innovation flourishes, and extraordinary results are possible.